They W
Real Brit

By MJ Wayland

"Maybe all the people who say ghosts don't exist are just afraid to admit they do."

Michael Ende, The Neverending Story

Paperback published 5th December 2015

Copyright © 2015 MJ Wayland

All rights reserved. No part of this publication may be reproduced, stored in a retrieval system, or transmitted, in any form or by any means without the prior written permission of the publisher, nor be otherwise circulated in any form of binding or cover other than that in which it is published and without a similar condition being imposed on the subsequent purchaser.

Author website:
www.mjwayland.com

CONTENTS

FOREWORD	5
KATE MIDDLETON'S GHOST	7
THE GHOST AND THE MURDERER	13
MYSTERY OF THE BLACK EYED CHILDREN	18
THE HAUGHTON CASTLE SPECTRE	26
THE VAMPIRES OF THE BORDERS	30
THE PHANTOM CANNONS OF HUMBERSIDE	33
LINCOLNSHIRE'S HAUNTED AIRFIELDS	36
LANCASHIRE'S MOST HAUNTED HOUSES	41
THE BISHOPTHORPE GHOST	46
THE GHOST SHIP	49
CLAPHAM WOODS : HAUNTED AND CURSED?	53
JAMES DURHAM'S FIGHT WITH A GHOST	58
GHOST OF THE POLISH AIRMAN	63
OXFORD'S HAUNTED COLLEGES	65
GHOSTS OF BALGONIE CASTLE	67
SCREAMING SKULLS	70
THE JORROCK'S SKULL	73
ROYALIST DEVIL OF WOODSTOCK MANOR	76
THE BRINKLOW HILL MYSTERIES	79
THE ISLE OF THE DEAD	87
THE PHANTOM HAND	92
SCOTLAND'S MOST HAUNTED ROAD	95
THE GHOST TOWN	98
TIME SLIPS	101
THE HAUNTED HANDS	106
A HAUNTING VILLAGE	109
RETURN OF GEOFFREY DE MANDEVILLE	112
YORK – BRITAIN'S MOST HAUNTED CITY	118
THE GHOSTS OF STREET HOUSE	124
THE OLD NURSING HOME	135
A to Z of BRITAIN'S SCARIEST GHOSTS	140
From the Author	159

FOREWORD

I believe in ghosts. I am now in my third decade of investigating and researching ghosts, am I any step nearer in finding the ultimate solution to the eternal questions, "do ghosts exist?"

Firstly, yes they do exist, every week many, many people believe they have witnessed a ghost, but under careful scrutiny I estimate nearly 95% of them could be explained in some way or another. Secondly, what about the 5% - what causes people to apparently meet disincarnate, seemingly intelligent 'ghosts'?

I have discussed thousands of cases with hundreds of witnesses, many are sincere and genuinely effected by the experiences, some stories push the limits of belief and a few seem to open the boundaries this world and the next. Ghost hunting is ultimately frustrating and rewarding in equal measure, however through twenty years plus of research and investigation I am more a sceptic and more of a believer than ever before! Being passionate but level-headed allows me to judge a case on the facts rather than my own beliefs, I approach cases purely open-minded and investigate as thoroughly as I can.

The cases in this book are a real mixture of stories that intrigue me – they excite, scare and bewilder and that makes for a great ghost story. You will find stories about Kate Middleton's ghost – how a tip off from a newspaper lead me to investigate the Middleton family's new home and the sad story of a broken marriage. Another favourite of mine is Brinklow Hill, a real place of mystery and hauntings, often left off the 'haunted places to visit' maps and overlooked, yet in the 1980s it was a real hot-bed of paranormal activity. And finally I reveal the truth behind the recent spate of Black-eyed children sightings in the UK and my thoughts on the phenomena.

If you love a good, authentic ghost story, then you will love these that I have personally selected for your enjoyment.

MJ Wayland
December 2014

KATE MIDDLETON'S GHOST

With reports of Kate Middleton's family moving to a new home – Bucklebury Manor in Berkshire, there have also been misconceptions that the home was haunted, when infact the Middleton will be moving next to one of the most haunted houses in Berkshire.

In May earlier this year many of the tabloid newspapers were full of stories of future queen Kate Middleton's parents moving to a new £4 million pound mansion in Berkshire. A Georgian building and Grade II listed, this slightly modern looking home sits next to Bucklebury House, once known as Bucklebury Old Manor.

Originally the Bucklebury Estate (and village) was owned by Reading Abbey however like many monasteries by 1538 the estate was confiscated and sold to John Winchcombe, the son of a wealthy woollen merchant, Jack O'Newbury. The original abbey building (on the site of Bucklebury House) was restructured by John and became the family seat of the Winchcombe family.

Our interest in Bucklebury Old Manor begins when the Winchcombes ran out of male heirs and the Estate passed to Lady Frances Winchcombe who married Henry St.John, Lord Bolingbroke, Secretary of State to Queen Anne.

Lady Frances was regarded as one of the most beautiful women of her age and indeed Henry St John was known for his handsome looks. Sadly it was an ill marriage, and within two years Henry was no longer living with Lady Frances. At the young age of thirty she retired to Bucklebury and set about rebuilding the kitchens and stables at Bucklebury Old Manor. Although practically living apart, the Bolingbrokes entertained Dean Swift, John Gay, Robert Harley and John Arbuthnot.

On 25th October 1718, Frances died at the tender age of 37, many claiming that she had died of a broken heart and/or her shock at her husband's actions. Since their marriage Henry St John became heavily involved in the politics of the country and wrongly for the time supported the Jacobite Rebellion. His actions (and words) forced him into exile in Paris, joining the Young Pretender. In 1716 he had lost his titles and estates and it was only in 1723 he was able to return and claim them back.

In 1832 Bucklebury Old Manor burnt down leaving a wing that was habitable but not at the standard of the Winchcombe family who moved to Lyegrove, the principal seat of their Sodbury Estates, some 12 miles north of Bath.

In the early 1900s, relations to the Winchcombes, the Webley-Parry family returned to Bucklebury village, and moved into a Georgian mansion called "The Cottages", they renamed the house "Bucklebury Manor" – this being the house that the Middleton's have recently purchased. The Webley-Parry's set about restoring the Old Manor and on completion called it "Bucklebury House". This may have caused confusion in the many reports of the Middleton's new home.

However the Middleton's have not only moved next to one of the most haunted houses in the village, but the village itself has a fair share of hauntings!
Just a little more than a hundred years after her death, locals believed that Lady Frances had began to walk the earth once again. Aside from being haunted by the Black Monks of the old abbey, the village of Bucklebury had gained a ghost.

And by 1898, another terrifying haunting was reported and this made several headlines in regional newspapers, this was in stark contrast to the usual media coverage of the political rallies, garden parties and horticultural meetings that took place at the Bucklebury Manor.

A Haunted House
News of the Old Manor's hauntings had reached the Falkirk Herald and on 20th August 1898 it printed an article titled "A Haunted House", after discussing the house's history the newspaper claimed:

> "Of course, the place is haunted and with two apparitions at least. A white lady walks the park and flits around the quiet pond; but a more terrible sight is the chariot drawn by six black horses mounted by headless positilions which at midnight issues from the portals of the ancient mansion, its ghostly wheels rattling on the uneven stones, and drives swiftly away to some

> fearsome destination. The stables, as they now stand, would seem to be indeed a fitting abode for the black steeds and the phantom coach, and it is not so long since that the family at the dwelling-house left hurriedly, scared away, so it is said by the ghostly tenants of the ruins."

Although correct in describing the Old Manor's alleged hauntings, I have yet to find evidence that any of the Webley-Parry family left the house in a hurry due to the phantom coach and horses.

Two years later the Reading Mercury mentioned the Old Manor and its hauntings in an article dated 18th August 1900,

> "The place is said to be haunted by Bolingbroke's wife who is supposed to walk here, and in some parts of the village towards the Common. Some of the villagers actually testify to having seen her."

However two years later at a time when the house was appearing in the news as a venue for various meetings and parties, The Reading Mercury published "The Story of Jack O'Newbury and the Winchcombes", a rollicking story of Lady Frances' relatives and its terrible hauntings.

> "Nothing now remains of the house at Bucklebury but the great kitchen with its wide open fireplace, the laundries, a small portion of the back of the house and part of the stables.

> The curious atmosphere of silence which hangs about the forsaken habitants of men pervades the place."

And then the Reading Mercury takes a leap that would change the manor's alleged hauntings seemingly forever.

> "Bucklebury must have been the scene of many searchings of the heart. One can imagine Lady Bolingbroke walking up and down the grass paths, and in the walled garden sad and solitary in her unhappy married life. Her ghost is said to haunt the place, a white lady in a chariot with black horses, driven by headless postilions. The old people of the village still tell the tale though they say that the chariot is never seen now."

With one printed article, the white lady is now seated in the chariot (which is apparently invisible as well) but still uses the same terms from the original Falkirk article, maybe it was misread by the journalist?

Modern interpretations built on the references from previous writers continue to mis-inform, for example this from the Berkshire History website:

> "Lady Bolingbroke's unhappy ghost is said to drive through the village in a coach drawn by the four black horses, often seen near the old fishponds, and on one night of the year she sits in the drawing-room of the Old Vicarage."

This statement shows a mixing of the "white lady wandering the ponds" story and now includes the coach and horses which is now transported to driving round ponds?!

Reference after reference claims that the white lady is seen in the carriage and wanders either the Old Manor's grounds or even the centre of Bucklebury village – and yet neither is reported in the original references.

Even in this day of multiple references via wikipedia and online archives errors in history are far too easy to make for the journalist and budding writer. The Middletons may not be moving into a well known haunted house (however the house is over two hundred years old so who knows?) but we know that the village of Bucklebury, a picturesque village of over a thousand years of history has some incredible hauntings and even more fascinating history.

References:
Falkirk Herald – Saturday 20 August 1898
Reading Mercury – Saturday 18 August 1900
Reading Mercury – Saturday 19 July 1902

THE GHOST AND THE MURDERER

> "It was believed that a female did appear, and always after midnight. Some soldiers refused duty at the post, some had been found lying on the ground through fright."

One of my favourite stories takes place in Drypool, Hull, one of the oldest areas of Hull that is even mentioned in the Domesday Book! With a rich history linked to the "Pilgrimage of Grace" - an uprising against King Henry VIII and the dissolution of the monasteries.

In an issue of the Leeds Mercury there was a letter signed by J.D. Bramley which is as follows:

"A few years ago after the Battle of Waterloo, our family removed from George Street, the centre of Hull, to Prospect Place in Drypool, which overlooked the green fields and the road leading to the garrison, a distance of 200 or 300 yards. It was our favourite resort to go and hear the band play and see the soldiers parade, and by our frequent visits we boys became acquainted with many of the men. The war being over many regiments came and went, Hull being a chief landing place, and when the 92nd Highlanders left, there came a foot regiment, but the number I forgot.

After a short time rumours were circulated in the new regiment respecting the appearance of a female - or the ghost of a female - at a certain sentry post at midnight. The rumours kept increasing to the dismay and terror of the soldiers and the town's folk, and the impression grew so strong among all classes, that the fact of a female appearing was not doubted. As the time passed the terror increased. Especially among those who were to amount guard at that particular post, which had obtained the objectionable name of 'Devils Post'. The stoutest hearts quailed and the guard was doubled.

Every morning great anxiety was felt to know in what new form or attitude the vision appeared - whether with a naked lighted candle or with a lantern? How many had seen her? How many soldiers had deserted, etc? In fact it the topic of our general conversation in Hull, but especially in Drypool.

Our friends and relatives, who were many, paid us almost daily visits from French's Gardens, from the district called Pottery Fields, from the Anlaby Road etc. The affair became quite a panic, and things seemed to be coming to a crisis.

At this time my eldest brother had been up early in the morning, and heard news that put all that had been seen and heard into the shade, and all of which was vouched to be true. After he had given us this news, it was decided that he and I should go to the garrison and see if we could test the truth of it. We set off at 11am to make the fullest enquiries. We soon entered the garrison and spoke to the sentry at the gate. He was armed and walking the monotonous twelve yard space. He answered us by referring us to the sentry at the far corner, for the information we wanted, I suppose he, being on duty, was not allowed to parley. We went as directed past the magazines and came to the post and was surprised to find the sentry in his box unarmed, in undress with his forage cap off and made some remark about it. We told him our errand, and said the sentry at the gate had referred us to him. He endeavoured to answer us in every particular.

Most of what we had previously heard was in the main true. It was firmly believed by them in the garrison that a female did appear, and always after change of guard at midnight. Some soldiers refused duty at the post, some had been found lying on the ground through fright and had been sent to the hospital. He told us that when the guard was doubled, the Sergeant, a powerful, stout man had volunteered to go on duty. When the form appeared that night the sentry asked the Sergeant if he could see her. He said no. The sentry placed his hand on his shoulder and the Sergeant, in fright, fell down and had to be taken away. He went on to say that things came to such a pass that the authorities had decided to thoroughly investigate. Accordingly the night previously, the garrison chaplain was prevailed upon, in company with a guard of six armed men. To 'pray her down' - as he termed it - including the man who had put his arm on the Sergeant, since he seemed to know more of the affair.

They went to the 'Devil's Post' at relief time – midnight. They had not long to wait; she did appear from the far corner with a lighted candle in her hand and, in silence, passed the group. The chaplain, he said, lost his courage, but he was roused by his companions, and ventured to open the book and say 'In the name of the

Father and of the Son and of the Holy Ghost, from whence art thou'? She beckoned with her hand and led the way. They followed the way she came - from the sentry box, past the first row of cavalry stables, round the corner, and down to the second row, a triangular corner, a secluded lonely spot at the North East corner of the garrison. Here she stopped, pointed to the ground where she stood and vanished into the earth.

The sentry said that they were all frightened and relieved when she had gone.

Early that morning, with spade and pickaxe, they set to work to dig up the spot where she had vanished. At about three feet or so they came upon the remains of a human form - all the bones of a skeleton. He told us, "it looks like a real grave; its not far off; just around the corner. If you would like to go and see, I'll go and show you" We both went with him to the desolate spot and there was the grave, sure enough, wide open. Heavy rain had fallen through the night and covered the bottom. I looked for the bones. I thought I saw some, but he said they had been, or would be gathered up,(I forgot which) to have the rites of a Christian burial. The pick and spade were there.

We took a look round, and made a few comments on what we heard, than bade good morning to relate what we had seen. We met others going to the scene for information. Doubtless there are, now living in Hull, many who can corroborate all that I have stated and perhaps more. The stout Sergeant I knew well, and the first time I saw him after his fright he was much altered. I had not the courage to ask him anything.

The next thing reported was that the man who had placed his hand on the sergeant was arrested and accused of murder. He confessed that about seven years before, when his regiment formed the garrison, he made acquaintance with a girl. They often met at the post, and from some cause he had murdered her and buried her where she was found.

During the excitement of this revelation, orders came for the removal of the regiment to march North - it was said to Newcastle or Durham. It was also rumoured that there, the culprit was tried on his own confession and paid the penalty. Such is the truth of what we saw and heard."

Research shows that the 33rd foot regiment, which was the only regiment to have served twice in Hull, was there first in 1811. Also a John Dearman in 1817 lived at No. 11 Prospect Place in Drypool. He was in fact a master mariner on the ship "Eliza", a Hull - London cheese monger vessel. So as fantastic as the story seems, there is an element in truth in the witness's story.

MYSTERY OF THE BLACK EYED CHILDREN

In September 2014, spectral children with black eyes began terrorising visitors and inhabitants of Cannock Chase in Staffordshire, UK. From an old pub to a walker's path in a forest, these children would disappear as promptly as they would appear.

Lee Brickley, a local researcher claimed he received the following report from one such witness,

> On Saturday 13th September, my wife and I were walking though Cannock Chase near to Stile Cop with our dog. Once we had entered the woodland, and the road was no longer visible, we started to hear the giggling noise of a little girl.
>
> To our amazement, a child, no taller than one meter in height appeared as if out of nowhere further up the path in front of us. We stopped dead in our tracks after noticing her eyes had no colour. Her head was tilted to the side in much the same way it would appear if she had been hung.
>
> She stared at us for around five minutes before running away into a densely grouped area of trees. My wife wanted to follow her, but I was having none of it.

In another article Lee claimed that he had received this report in July 2013,

We instantly started running towards the noise...we couldn't find the child anywhere and so stopped to catch our breath.

That's when I turned round and saw a girl stood behind me, no more than 10 years old, with her hands over her eyes.

It was as if she was waiting for a birthday cake.

I asked if she was OK and if she had been the one screaming. She put her arms down by her side and opened her eyes.

That's when I saw they were completely black, no iris, no white, nothing.

I jumped back and grabbed my daughter. When I looked again, the child was gone. It was so strange.

By the 2nd October, a local pub in financial difficulties and up for sale, claimed that it was haunted by the Black Eye Child. The Daily Star published this account,

> The Four Crosses is a former coaching inn that dates back to the 17th century. It has been put on the market for £325,000, but even the low price has failed to tempt anyone.
>
> The previous owners have now left. They tried to cash in on its notoriety by holding special ghost

hunts, with a paranormal TV investigation once being filmed there. They concluded it was the most haunted building they had ever visited.

It all sounds very strange, is there really a re-awakening of a ghost that is now stalking Cannock Chase and a Pub?

To understand what is happening here we need to look at the Black Eyed Children phenomenon and we need to start in the U.S.A.

For the last fifteen years there have been reports of black-eyed children in America, all portraying similar behaviour as the Cannock Chase 'ghost'. Many researchers have looked into the historic value of these hauntings, and it is only during research that the truth comes to light. While there are plenty of mentions of these types of ghosts on the internet and modern day books - sightings stop at 1998. Why aren't there any sightings of such ghosts in the U.S. before this time.

The reason is that it was a hoax.

The great resource, Skeptoid.com, wrote this about the black-eyed children,

> The earliest published account that anyone's been able to find was posted to the Usenet newsgroup alt.magick on July 30, 1997, by Brian Bethel, a newspaper spirituality columnist in Abilene, Texas. He also posted the same story a month later in alt.folklore.ghost-stories, with an

additional epilogue about how he spoke to some friends afterward who reported a similar experience. Bethel's original account was lengthy, but here's a heavily edited overview:

I drove by the theater on the way into the center proper and pulled into an empty parking space. Using the glow of the marquee to write out my check, I was startled to hear a knock on the driver's-side window of my car. I looked over and saw two children staring at me from [the] street... Both were boys, and my initial impression was that they were somewhere between 10-14... I rolled down the window very, very slightly and asked "Yes?" The spokesman smiled again, broader this time. His teeth were very, very white. "Hey, mister, what's up? We have a problem," he said... His command of language was incredible and he showed no signs of fear. He spoke as if my help was a foregone conclusion... "C'mon, mister," the spokesman said again, smooth as silk... "Now, we just want to go to our house. And we're just two little boys." That really scared me. Something in the tone and diction again sent off alarm bells... "C'mon, mister. Let us in. We can't get in your car until you do, you know," the spokesman said soothingly... For the first time, I noticed their eyes. They were coal black. No pupil. No iris. Just two staring orbs reflecting the red and white light of the marquee. At that point, I know my expression betrayed me... "WE CAN'T COME IN UNLESS YOU TELL US IT'S

OKAY. LET ... US .... IN!"... I ripped the car into reverse (thank goodness no one was coming up behind me) and tore out of the parking lot. I noticed the boys in my peripheral vision, and I stole a quick glance back. They were gone.

So the first ever black-eyed children ghosts, were actually boys!

Later that day Bethel published a lengthy reply to another posting, this time about a childhood game called, "Bloody Mary": if you go up to a mirror at midnight in the dark and say "Bloody Mary" three times, then she will appear to you in the mirror. Bethel posed the question whether a fictitious entity might actually become real, driven by the power of belief.

Is this Bethel admitting he had created the black-eye children story? Either way his story quickly made its rounds on various boards and forums, and soon others claimed they had seen black-eyed children of both sexes. However it took a popular movie to really create the ghost seen today.

In 2002, the American version of the Japanese horror movie "Ring" was released. The premise is that somewhere "out there" exists a cursed videotape, anyone who watches the tape receives a mysterious phone call and dies seven days later. The movie's plot follows the investigation into the images depicted on the video tape and the appearance of "Samara Morgan" who was pushed down a well and died seven days later.

Samara is a vengeful ghost and appears with dark, wet black hair covering her face and wearing a tattered short-sleeved dress and black shoes. Her skin is an unnatural mouldy colour, and her eyes are colourless (but not black).

Since its release Black-eyed children hoax stories have become intertwined with the appearance of the Ring ghost. And indeed it was only a matter of time before the Cannock Chase ghost had its own hoaxers. Within days of the original reports being published two people came forward with suspect photographs of the 'ghost'.

On 15th October, Michelle Mason submitted to the Stoke Sentinel a photograph of her children in Cannock Chase - with an obvious fake ghost created using a popular smart phone app. Michelle claimed that the photograph was taken on a digital camera, and yet the ghost appearing on her photo was definitely one from an easily downloadable app.

A day later medium Christine Hamlett claimed she had photographed the black-eyed child ghost, her photograph appearing in The Mirror newspaper. All would be well and good, except that I have received dozens of fake photographs sent by email from Christine over the last three years. Even if her Cannock Chase ghost photo is "real" - her previous claims to me that she has photographed the ghosts of Elvis, Princess Diana and Jim Morrison in her home, throw doubt on her most recent claim.

And with that the story died in most of the newspapers, except for the highly unreliable Daily Star which continued to publish stories up to Halloween with titles such as, "Black-eyed child ghost sends house prices plummetting", "Never mind Halloween, Black-eyed ghost invasion on 27th October" and "Black-eyed monster clowns set to target UK's roads at nights".

So were people really seeing the black-eyed child ghost, or was it a demon as many newspapers claimed during the two week burst of stories? My thoughts are that with all these stories, except for the hoax photographs, all the witness statements come from one person: Lee Brickley. Surprisingly for an alleged researcher, why are there no detailed descriptions of the ghost in both sightings? What colour is the girls hair? What clothes was she wearing? Was she wearing shoes? Etc.Etc.

It sounds pretty incomprehensible that a researcher would allow descriptions to fall by the wayside. Either Lee received these cases anonymously, and therefore could be hoaxes or Lee hoaxed them himself. Further more Lee makes incredible claims about the ghost sightings in Cannock Chase and starting the "demonic child" rumours in the press. Lee wrote this about his thoughts,

> However, we know that Satanists like to conjure up demons, and which entities are their number one preference? You guessed it – Child Demons. (I have researched for many years alleged Satanism in the UK and interviewed

Satanists but have not read one account where they were trying to raise a 'child demon' – MJ)

Demonic Children are, for the most part, considered to be the offspring of upper-level evil entities (although some are demon/human hybrids). They look like mortal children but are described as pure evil. Generally regarded as extremely dangerous, their powers are known to become even stronger with age. Take for example "Cambion", also known as "The Devils Brat", who, in medieval England, often took the form of a devious child, leading unknowing victims on a wild goose chase, frequently resulting in their death from a steep fall or something of the like: sound familiar?

Lee is making massive presumptions based on little knowledge with the two paragraphs above. The latter paragraph sounds like he's making it up as he goes along - maybe that is his intention - to create a series of hoaxes or notoriety for himself? Considering that it was only last year Lee was claiming in national newspapers that there had been sightings of Pig-Headed Men and Wolf-Men in Cannock Chase - who do you believe?

THE HAUGHTON CASTLE SPECTRE

Haughton Castle sits on the pretty banks of the North Tyne and is a well-known area for fine trout fishing. With a history dating to over a thousand years, the castle is likely to have been built out of stone used for Hadrian's Wall. With this incredible history is there any doubt it should be haunted?

The castle overbears the neighbouring village of Barrasford and is an impressive building. The castle, similar in design to the fourteenth century tower built at nearby Chillingham, is inhabited and parts of the castle have been modernised but who is the infamous Haughton Castle Ghost?

The following ghost story occurs during the time when the 'Border Reivers' or 'Mosstroopers' would attack English land, quite legally and then return to their tribes in Scotland. It was a time when villagers, tribes and families battled each other for food and 'treasure'.

Sir John de Widderington, at that time was the Lord of Haughton Castle and known for being a good and gallant person who fought for peace during the Border battles. During Sir John's rule at Haughton, the King appointed weak-willed Lord Dacre of Gilsland as Lord Warden of the Marches. The task of the warden was to ensure peace on the Borders and deal with troublemaker tribes such as the Armstrongs and Kerrs, as well as the Scots from the North. It was only a matter of time before Dacre began to accept bribes, ignoring the troubles and causing the law to collapse.

Dacre, to make matters worse courted a female of the notorious Armstrong clan, the very sister of the leader of this murdering family troop of reivers. On hearing this news, local landowners formed an alliance to protect their rights and report Dacre's deeds to the King.

While Cardinal Wolsley visited York, Sir John decided to meet with Wolsley with two delegates from the landowners association. On the night before the meeting, Sir John's men fought and captured a reiver rustling cattle in the local meadows. The Lord put the man in his dungeon at Haughton Castle, so he could deal with him when he returned.

To reach York by horse in Sir John's days took two days of hard riding. On arrival to the city, Sir John realised he had the key of the dungeon in his pockets and that worse still he had neglected to leave instructions with his staff to feed or water his prisoner.

In a state of desperation and fear, Sir John turned his horse around and headed back to Haughton Castle, by the time he reached Durham, his steed dropped dead with exhaustion. When he reached his castle forty-eight hours later he feared the worse.

"How fared the prisoner?" Sir John asked his servants.

The servants replied that the man cried and moaned, then he began to scream but the noise died down, and nothing had been heard since.

Sir John unlocked the cell and found the reiver dead.

The spirit of the prisoner returned to haunt the castle months later, night after night the sounds of the prisoner cries and moans would echo around the surrounding countryside. The screams would keep awake Sir John and his staff through the night. Servants left the service of Sir John and the village of Barrasford demanded that he take action.

The Rector of Simonburn was called in to exorcise the ghost; this he did immediately and nothing was heard no more. To comfort Sir John, the Rector left with him the Black-lettered Bible from which he read during the exorcism.

Curiously, when the Bible was sent to London for re-binding the reiver's moaning and screams returned to haunt Haughton Castle. Orders were given to return the Bible quickly from London and lay the spirit of the ghost once again.

Interestingly in the 1970s Paul Devereux discovered while researching his ground breaking book "The Ley Hunter's Companion" that a ley line runs through the village of Barrasford and on to Haughton Castle.

Further more that in the 1800s Barrasford's village inn burned to the ground in a mysterious fire that killed one of the villagers. Over the years many visitors to the area have witnessed the sighting of a burning man running through the fields running from Barrasford to Haughton.

I have written before about the trackways of ghosts and this is an even more intriguing insight into "field theory" (my own belief on how ghosts work) – how or why are ghosts such as the burning man following ley lines or why does the Repton monk follow the line of an alleged tunnel? Here we seem to be swinging to and fro from local consciousness (the tunnel) and earth energy (ley line) – could there possibly be a link between the two?

THE VAMPIRES OF THE BORDERS

Stories of vampirism are rife in all the countries that make up the United Kingdom. Scotland and England have very prolific stories of the vampire and that is no different for the towns that are situated on the Scottish/England border.

The Croglin Vampire case claimed that during the Victorian times a bout of vampirism occurred in a quiet village just thirty miles from the Scottish border, this has been discussed further on this website. Vampires were not restricted to Eastern Europe, as we already know but there were Vampires close to the two border towns of Berwick and Melrose.

The Canon William of Newburgh, a highly respected priest who lived during the reign of Richard I in the thirteenth century, introduced the tale of the Berwick Vampire to folklore. This was the time when plague devastated whole towns and cities in one swoop and the northern counties were no exception.

William's story concerns a rich merchant who was a victim of the plague but was known as a religious, thoughtful man. Only after his death did the villagers of Berwick discover that the man had lead a corrupt, sinful life and they denied his burial on consecrated land. Soon after his funeral, inexplicable and terrible incidents took place in Berwick. The merchant had begun to rise from his grave in search of human flesh and blood amongst the villagers. The demented demon would bolt through the streets looking for victims shouting, "Until my body is burnt, you folk of Berwick shall have no peace!" Behind the Vampire a pack of howling dogs followed him, their loud baying keeping villagers awake.

The villagers had to end the horror of the Vampire and decided to meet. Ten young farmhands were selected to exhume the merchant's grave and dismember the body and burn it until only ashes remained.

But tragedy would not go away, shortly after the destruction of the vampire, the plague returned to Berwick levelling half the population. Villagers claimed as they buried their dead that the sound of baying hounds and the fearful screams of the Vampire could be heard.

Canon William also introduced the similar tale of Vampirism that happened in Melrose. The vampire in this case was the "Hundeprest" a priest who enjoyed the material pleasures of life and hunting.

After the priest had died, his former mistress would complain that his loud moans and groans haunted her bedchamber. The church decided to help and sent four monks to despatch the ghost. The monks kept vigil at the priests grave to see if he would rise again. In the days before street lighting the monks sat in darkness, with only the half giving light in the autumn night. The monks expected the Hundeprest to emerge during the witching hour but the hour passed without incident. Chilled to the bone, three monks sought warmth from a nearby cottage.

No sooner had they left the Hundeprest attacked the remaining monk but in the form of a terrible monster. The monk stood his ground as the Hundeprest charged towards him. The monk side-stepped the vampire and swung his axe, driving it deep into the demon. The monster groaned and fled into the night with the brave monk in pursuit. Soon they reached the grave, where the vampire disappeared back in to its grave.

As dawn broke the other monks returned, shocked to hear what had happened, they decided to open up the grave. As they dug, blood seeped through the ground and when the corpse was finally revealed, the corpse looked fresh apart from a huge gaping, bleeding wound. The monks took the corpse away from the monastery and burned it to ashes.

THE PHANTOM CANNONS OF HUMBERSIDE

There are many reports worldwide detailing the sounds of "phantom cannons" or "ghostly gun-fire". Over the years I have uncovered many such accounts buried within old literature, during a visit to Bradford Central Library I discovered a case of "Phantom Cannons" in 1658.

Researcher and author, Charles Fort wrote about the "Guns of Barisal", a series of incidents during the 1890's that were thought to be cannon-fire and yet Hull's "Phantom Cannons" took place over two hundred years earlier.

> "The true relation of a strange and very wonderful thing that was heard in the air October 12th, 1658, by hundreds of people.
>
> Now I come to relate the matter, the which was thus: Upon the 12th day of October, in the afternoon, there was heard by some hundreds of people in Holderness, Hedon, and about Hull, and several other places in Yorkshire first, three great pieces of ordnance or cannons discharged in the air one after another, very terrible to hear, and afterwards immediately followed a peal of muskets. This shooting off of muskets continued about an half-quarter of an hour, drums beating all the while in the manner just as if two armies had been engaged. Such as heard the aforesaid cannons, muskets, and drums, do report that the sound was from the north-east

quarter, and, to their thinking not far from the place where they stood.

Two men being together about six miles from Hull in Holderness, near Humber-side, supposed it was directly over Hull; whereupon one said to the other, "It being the sheriff's riding-day at Hull, this peal of muskets must be there; and see (quoth he) how the smoke riseth!" Now the reason why he mentioned the smoke was, because no sooner was this noise finished over Hull, but (as it happeneth after the discharge of guns) there arose a very great smoke or thick mist round about the town, although immediately before (the day being very clear day, and the sun shining all the while bright) he saw the town very perfectly.

One thing more was observed by him who saw the smoke over Hull; that all the while this prodigious noise continued (which was as he supposed, about the eighth part of an hour), the face of the sky (as in the eclipse of the sun) waxed very dim; yea, such tremble and quake under him.

A certain gentleman, who had been some time a major in the war, as he was riding with a friend between the towns of Patterington and Ottringham, was so persuaded that some encounter by soldiers was on the other side of a small hill where they were riding, as that they could not but mount the hill to try the truth, so plainly did the drums beat and the muskets go off, and, to their thinking, so near them, as either it must be a sign from heaven or a real battle hard by.

The country people were struck with such strange wonder and deep terror, that they gave over their labour, and ran home with fear; yea, some poor people gathering coals by the seaside were so frightened that they ran away leaving their sacks behind them. In conclusion: for the space of forty miles this fearful noise of cannons, muskets, and drums was heard all the country over."

LINCOLNSHIRE'S HAUNTED AIRFIELDS

A faint throb of a Lancaster returning in the morning mist, a light flickers in a disused control tower and a roar of laughter comes from the derelict pilot's quarters. The ghosts of Britain's abandoned airfields have intrigued investigators for years. These ghostly tales are from people who have experienced a close brush with the supernatural in some of Britain's most eeriest places.

There are at least eight books that detail the appearances and habits of ghosts at Lincolnshire's airfields, whether derelict or not. What attracts people to read these books is the reality behind the stories, often very sad or heart-warming but most of all chilling.

Waltham's Ghostly Airman
The Royal Air Force quickly abandoned many airfields after war, RAF Waltham, near Grimsby is one such airfield.

RAF Waltham was opened as a heavy-bomber station with squadrons of Wellington Bombers stationed there. While stationed at Waltham, No. 100 squadron attacked targets across Germany and the occupied countries of Europe. In 1945 the station closed and the No.35 maintenance unit used the airfield for storage but this wasn't for long and they too left.

According Bruce Halpenny in "Ghost Stations" late in 1969, Susan Burchell lived on the perimeter of the airfield, and her house was built on the foundations of old wartime huts. One night, Susan awoke to see in the gloom, somebody standing at the foot of her bed. She switched on her bedside lamp and clearly saw the figure of a young ginger haired airman in uniform, with one sleeve pinned to his shoulder.

The phantom airman continued to stare at Burchell before moving slowly towards her wardrobe and disappearing into it.

Susan began to scream and awoke her parents. They began to search the house and garden, including the wardrobe but found nothing. Although the airman never appeared again, the family soon moved out.

Local folklore claims that the hut which Burchell's house was built over was destroyed when an ex-crew member who had done many missions, and been declared unfit for flying, due to injuries caused in an attack, killed himself with an hand-grenade.

Other airmen have been seen walking around the airstrip, once a popular area for courting couples. In 1982, a phantom airman was seen walking up and down before vanishing into the darkness. A memorial for the No.100 squadron situated on a nearby road also has a phantom airman who appears regularly.

RAF Metheringham's Phantom Lady
Although little remains of RAF Metheringham, its ghost continues to remind people that it played an important role in World War 2.

A young lady, in her late teens is often spotted standing at the side of the road between 9:30 and 10:00pm. She stands on what was once part of the airfield and wears a pale green coat with a grey scarf. Pinned to her lapel is a RAF wings badge. The ghost has stopped cyclists, motorists and pedestrians, asking for help, telling whoever she stops that her fiancé has skidded riding his motorcycle and is lying injured nearby. The ghost appears quite real rather than the ethereal. As with most road ghosts, there is a sinister side to the sighting. On her sudden disappearance, the witness is stricken with inexplicable fear, panic and sense of unreality. The ghost leaves behind a powerful odour of putrefaction. One witness who met the lady said, "I could not see her eyes, or horribly, no eyes in the sockets at all, the frontal skull orbits were empty!"

Halpenny claims that the young lady was killed near the end of World War 2 when her fiancé crashed his bike, throwing her off it, and breaking her neck and causing terrible head injuries. The two were due to be married and she had just ordered her wedding gown.

The Most Haunted Airfield?
RAF Elsham Wold opened in July 1941; similar to Waltham, as a heavy bomber station and from the outset it held Wellingtons, Halifaxes and finally Lancaster Bombers. Elsham Wold is a cold bleak site and the squadrons based there had many losses and accidents caused by ice and freezing fog.

In January 1945, Corporal Hilary, took a van across the far side of the airfield, due to the thick fog, Hilary had to drive with the van lights full on. It was midday and Hilary became lost out on the airfield. She stepped out of the van to try and locate her position, when she saw coming out of the fog into the van headlights three aircrew in full flying kit. She asked them for directions but they just walked past and disappeared into the fog. That day no flying took place because of the fog and aircrew would not have walked across the field. Did Hilary see a phantom crew?

The airfield closed in 1947 and a new road cuts through the airfield. For many years the Gregory family lived in the wartime control tower at Elsham Wold. They often heard mysterious morse code messages and saw phantom airmen walking around their home.

Their first experiences came as soon as they moved into the tower. A tapping noise could be heard on one of the walls, the noise continued for months and the Gregorys realised that there was a pattern to the tapping. When ex-servicemen visited the tower, they told the Gregorys that it was in fact morse code.

As with most haunted airfields, a phantom airman kept the family spooked. The airman would appear at the bottom of Mr and Mrs Gregory's bed, smile and then disappear. One night he was seen by Mr Gregory sitting in one of their chairs smiling once again, when Gregory moved, the airman stood up and disappeared.

Another incident involved the Gregorys' son, Paul. One night, Mrs Gregory heard her son screaming in the middle of the night.

"When I went in his room, he was sitting up in bed screaming his head off," she said. "He said 'Can't you hear that plane? It's talking off and it's not coming back.

Paul described in great detail a four-engined aircraft and its seven-man crew he had seen taking off from the old main runaway, which is less than 100 yards from his bedroom window in the control tower.

Today, the tower no longer exists, demolished to make way for a new road from the M180 and the Humber Bridge. The road also follows the line of one of Elsham Wold's runways – so one foggy night you might meet one of its phantom aircrews.

LANCASHIRE'S MOST HAUNTED HOUSES

Dramatic and often short lives were lived by some of Lancashire's most powerful and religious families. In the face of adversity of religious persecution or for just downright love, these families are known as much for being haunters and less of the haunted.

The Walls of Chingle Hall
Just off the Goosnargh to Whittingham Lane, is one of the most haunted and wrote about houses in Lancashire, Chingle Hall is a cross-shaped house, it was built by the de Singletons about 1260, surrounded by a moat and approached over a low bridge.

The Singletons lived in the Hall until 1585 when an heiress married into the Wall family. Here the family lived and in the room over the porch a son was born, destined to be St John Wall. Life in his childhood was difficult, the Walls being Papist and compelled to send John to Douai for his education by the Jesuits.

Years later he returned, as a Franciscan missioner. He moved around the West Midlands and was eventually executed at Worcester in 1679, becoming a martyr. His severed head disappeared allegedly secretly returned to his birthplace.

The ghost of a male cloaked figure is often seen in the birth chamber of St John Wall and the door has an unnerving habit of opening and closing. The figure has been witnessed crossing the bridge, entering the porch and ascending the stairs and manifesting its presence by rappings and tappings. Often it causes flowers to shake in their vases, pictures to dance on the wall and the occasional dislodgement of objects.

The hall also has strange currents of air – icy cold breezes in warm rooms and smoke issuing from unexpected places.

Recent investigations of the Hall by the BBC were unsuccessful, for whatever reason recording equipment refused to work but a tape recorder captured approximately sixty seconds of anomalous screaming from the Hall.

The Southworths of Samlesbury Hall
The ghost of Samlesbury Hall is that of Dorothy Southworth, the daughter of an "Obnoxious Papist Family" as described on the official roll call of Papists in 1590's. Samlesbury Hall was always under close surveillance by the government, often searched for evidence of forbidden masses and hidden priests.

Dorothy's tale is that of forbidden love – a love affair with the son of a protestant family. She was due to elope with her love when her brothers discovered her treachery and promptly killed her love and his friend. In the 1820's the remains of two men were unearthed during road making near the Hall's moat.

Dorothy, heart-broken and maddening with grief was sent to a nunnery, where she died.

Since her death, a White Lady appears near the Hall often stopping passing motorists of the A59. She also appeared to an Amateur Acting Group performing nearby! Her activities include visiting the caretaker's house often appearing next to his bed. Dorothy being on of the most busiest ghosts, also walks along a path between the Hall and the road, one night during World War 2, two soldiers saw her – causing one of them to faint and the other run!

The Osbaldestons
Less than two miles from the Southworths is Osbaldeston, the name of the old family who intermittently carried feuds with their neighbours at Samlesbury Hall. Both families were Papists, but the Osbaldestons held relations with Queen Elizabeth I and the Southworth's were not happy about this.

In 1593, Edward Osbaldeston returned to Lancashire after tuition from Jesuits, as a missioner. Unfortunately, he was soon caught and executed. His brother, as head of the family mended the feud with the Southworth family by marrying his son Thomas to a Southworth daughter. After this happy event, followed a tragic one.

Thomas's sister Elizabeth had married Edward Walsh, even though Thomas disagreed with her choice of partner. We do not know the source of their differences but one night when Edward Walsh returned home, he was involved in a duel with Thomas. Both fought in the room where they quarrelled and both swords were drawn. Walsh fell to the ground with blood gushing from a deep chest wound.

The blood soaked into the floorboards as he laid dying, and to this day no amount of washing or scrubbing has ever been able to remove the stain. If you visit Osbaldeston Hall today the mark still remains!

A ghost often appears, moaning and exposing the wound while staggering through the hall.

The Norris Family of Speke Hall
The Norris family built their mansion eight miles from the then tiny fishing village of Liverpool in 1490.

Little did they realise that 500 years later their home would be surrounded by a modern industrial estate and Liverpool Airport. By 1612 the house had been extended to include a central courtyard, a Tudor Great Hall, richly plastered ceilings, fine carvings and a moat. The Hall stands in a wooded park by the Mersey.

Speke Hall is a magnificent mansion grouped around a courtyard where two 500-year-old yew trees called Adam and Eve flourish.

For many generations the Norris family lived at Speke Hall. In penal times so much activity took place here due to this being a convenient spot for the reception of returning Jesuit missioners and priests. A lot of ghost activity should occur at Speke Hall, but it only has one ghost, that of the last Norris, an heiress called Mary.

Mary had married the younger son of the Duke of St Albans, a descendant of Charles II and Nell Gwynn, but he was a no-good person and was a spendthrift.

Driven to madness by her husband's behaviour, she snatched her baby from the cradle and, not knowing her actions, hurled the infant from the window of the tapestry room into the moat below. In that haunted room the cradle gently rocks and no hand is visible. Mary Norris ended her own life in the Great Hall downstairs, set to wander Speke Hall for an eternity.

THE BISHOPTHORPE GHOST

And now a tale from the outskirts of York at the village famed for it's palace, Bishopthorpe. The most veritable ghost was the one which was supposed to be the ghost of Archbishop Scrope, who for many years walked the road to conduct his own funeral procession. Perhaps the most persistent story told of his appearance was that told by a man who made his living as a slaughterman, he used to speak with confidence of what he saw.

> "Robert Johnson, accompanied by a boy who was apprenticed to a Jubbergate butcher was sent one night in the 1800s to a farm beyond Bishopsthorpe to fetch some sheep. As they returned in the darkness, nearing the hauling land, each suddenly saw a coffin suspended in the air, and moving slowly along in the direction of York.
>
> It tilted occasionally, as if borne on the shoulders of men who were thrown out of step by the rugged character of the roadway. The coffin was covered with a heavy black pall of velvet, fringed with white silk, and was in size and appearance the resting-place of a full grown man.
>
> Behind it, with measured tread, walked a Bishop in lawn, bearing on his hands a large open book, over which his head bent, but from his lips no sound came. On went the procession, with the

steady precision observed in bearing the dead to the grave, whilst the sheep kept pace, and would not be driven past the strange sight. Nobody could be mistaken in the apparition. The night, through dark, was too light to admit of mistake.

The spectre procession moved at a leisured pace for some considerable distance till it came to the field where the Archbishop was beheaded. Then it disappeared as hastily as it had come, and returned to its rest. But not so with the man and boy, having arrived at their destination after very few particulars, spoken amid much fear, they were taken off to bed, where they remained for many days, wrung in mind and body by the terrible shock.

When sufficiently recovered, their story was repeated with particular detail, and gained universal credence, from the fact many villagers and many citizens had experienced the sight and sensation. The boy forsook his business and took to the sea, lest he should ever gain be compelled to take a similar journey, and be subject to like experience, whilst the man ever after avoided that road at nightfall, but never swerved from declaring his story true. More than once after this, men who had sat late at their cups were frightened into sobriety by the reappearance of the strange funeral procession, but the ghost has done its work, for in our day it never appears."

A tale that is still told in Bishopthorpe and the surrounds, indeed during World War II it was said that Scrope was "walking again", and could be seen on moonlit nights as the bombers flew off to Germany.

THE GHOST SHIP

> "During the evening of February 13th, 1748, the schooner Lady Luvibond, loaded with a general cargo for Oporto, and under the command of Captain Simon Reed, sailed down the Thames.."

The wreck of the Lady Luvibond is persistent Goodwin Sands ghost story. The Goodwin Sands is a ten mile long sandbank in the English Channel, lying off the Kent coast of England. Due to the nature of tides and currents in the area, the bank is constantly shifting, causing many shipwrecks.

It is believed that there have been more than two thousand ships wrecked on the sands, including the HMS Stirling Castle in 1703, VOC ship Rooswijk in 1740, the SS Montrose in 1914, and the South Goodwin Lightship, which broke free from its anchor moorings during a storm in 1954. There have also been several naval battles found nearby including the Battle of Goodwin Sands in 1652, and the Battle of Dover Strait in 1917. However Goodwin Sands is haunted by the Lady Luvibund, a ghost ship that reappears every fifty years.

During the evening of February 13th, 1748, the schooner Lady Luvibond, loaded with a general cargo for Oporto, and under the command of Captain Simon Reed, sailed down the Thames to safely clear the North Foreland. Captain Reed was particularly happy on this trip, for he had his new wife aboard along with her mother and their wedding guests. On deck, however, while the guests were drinking toasts to the newly married couple in the captain's cabin below, first mate, John Rivers, who had been a rival for the affections of Simon Reed\'s wife, nursed his hatred and jealousy.

A fair wind blew that night and the Lady Luvibond sped across the water. But, as he stood in the wind, something must have snapped in John River's mind. He walked casually aft and drew a heavily wooden belaying-pin from a rack. Deliberately he strolled towards the helmsmen and, pretending to peer over the man's shoulder at the binnacle, River's shattered the poor sailors skull with the belaying pin. Rolling the lifeless body into the scuppers, Rivers took the helm and swung the Lady Luvibond hard over.

In the captain's cabin the bridal party still made merry, too pre-occupied to notice the ship's change of course, until, with a grinding crash, the schooner hit the Goodwin Sands. The masts snapped and toppled into the sea, and the timbers rent like matchwood with ear-splitting groans. Down in the cabin the captain and his guests were trapped and helpless. Above the din of the dying ship rose the hideous cacophony of River's revengeful laughter.

By first light on February 14th, 1748, the Lady Luvibond had been sucked into the Goodwin Sands forever. At the subsequent court of enquiry John River's mother gave evidence that she had heard her son say he would get even with Simon Reed if it cost him his life.

The case of the Lady Luvibond was logged as misadventure.

Fifty years later to the day, Captain James Westlake, aboard the coasting vessel Eldridge, was skirting the edge of Goodwin Sands, when he caught sight of a three-masted schooner bearing down on him with sails set. Shouting to the helmsman to slam the Eldridge's wheel hard over, Westlake watched the other vessel sheer past. As it did so, Westlake heard the sound of female voices and merrymaking coming from the ships lower decks.

Reporting the incident to the ships owners, Westlake discovered that the crew of a fishing vessel had seen the same schooner go ashore on the Goodwins, to break up before their eyes. Making to rescue any survivors, the crew of the fishing vessel found nothing but empty sand and water. The Lady Luvibond had made her first phantom appearance.

On February 13 1848, Deal Hovellers watched the spectral Lady Luvibond go aground once again. They too set out to rescue but they found nothing. Again on February 13 1898, shore watchers saw the Lady Luvibond re-enact her pile up on the Goodwin Sands. They launched off, but found no trace of the wreck.

Other ships at sea have seen the Lady Luvibond go aground, and, during early January 1948, the 2,327 ton Italian vessel Silvia Onorato was wrecked on the Goodwins, some said that this time the Lady Luvibond had demanded a live sacrifice for her anniversary.

Consistently, the locals point out, every fifty years, on the exact anniversary of her doom, the phantom Lady Luvibond has re-enacted the consequences of a madman's deed of violence. On February 13th 1998, the fog was too thick for an appearance to be seen, however you will have to wait until 2048 to see if she manifests on her three hundredth anniversary.

CLAPHAM WOODS : HAUNTED AND CURSED?

Nestling in the shelter of the South Downs in West Sussex, is a small village surrounded by dense woodlands that harbour chilling and unusual activity. In 2003 Living TV's "Scream Team" visited the area causing interest in the paranormal community but most researchers won't know about the real strange incidents that kicked started long term investigations.

Clapham Woods has always been known as being a bit "weird" and what causes this is unknown. UFO's, ghosts and possible occult connotations all seem to occur in this quite small area.

The atmosphere of the woods is almost felt immediately with its strange looking, stunted trees and then there is the large crater. Was it caused by a wartime bomb or was it a meteorite – many believe that the reason nothing grows there is that it was an ancient lime pit but others believe it has a far darker explanation.

In the 1700's an old woman saw a "bright round shape like the full Moon" float down into the woods and disappear in the bushes, then the woods were filled with fumes that "stinketh of burning matter". The old woman was then struck down "smitten with palsy", and was given a wide berth by the locals.

Since then there has been a continuation of UFO sightings and possible landings. There have been many sightings reported to the police and investigators but there must be many more that have not reported for fear of ridicule.

A saucer-shaped object was witnessed by an insomniac while glancing out of his kitchen window in 1968. It was 2am and he saw the object hovering directly over the nearby woods. He immediately called the police who when they arrived, the UFO had disappeared.

In October 1972, a telephone engineer driving home alone along Findon Road saw a large-saucer shaped object in the sky before making a circle of the area before zooming off. Another report came from a couple walking near Long Furlong who thought they saw Venus low in the western sky until it started moving north very quickly. When the object was over Clapham Wood a beam of light descended vertically from it and then rapidly withdrew before shooting away to the North-East.

In 1967, in the village Rushington a few miles away, two schoolboys, Toyne Newton and John Arnold had a strange story spelled out to them on a ouija board. The message claimed that the woods were used as a base for spacecraft, and that one had landed to fetch supplies of sulphur and other chemicals. Unknown to them a few months earlier, Paul Glover witnessed a multiple UFO sighting that seemed to show exactly what the message had said.

In 1975 reports of disappearing dogs in the woods began to flood in to the Worthing Herald, a local newspaper. Wallace, a three year old chow disappeared, as did a two year old collie belonging to John Cornford. The collie, normally obedient suddenly rushed into a small copse between two trees and was never seen again, although its mystified owner searched the area thoroughly.

Another dog owner reported that when she took her dog in to the woods it ran round in circles, foaming at the mouth, with its eyes bulging out of its head as if in great pain. Luckily she was able to get it back into the car and home, where it calmed down.

Other animal owners have reported similar experiences. A horseman tethered his mount while he relieved himself, he was amazed to find the animal disappeared during his brief absence, he made exhaustive enquiries but the horse was never found.

As with most strange areas there seems to be a strange electro-magnetic/static charge which seems to affect people entering the woods or even causing effects such as advanced decomposition on a man who had died in the woods after disappearing two weeks earlier. It was something the pathologist couldn't explain.

Dave Stringer of Southern Paranormal Investigation Group decided to visit the woods in August 1977 to check out the stories. While he was there he witnessed a dark shape about 12 feet high, while it was not a bush or tree, he could only describe it as a "Black Mass". This linked directly with an increase in radiation recorded by the Geiger counter that he took with him. During the sighting, in the distance, a white disc shot out of the woods into the sky disappearing at the same time as the black mass. Stringer retraced his footsteps towards where the form had appeared and he found a four toed footprint, twice the width of a man's foot but very narrow at the heel.

Only on one other occasion has he seen such a footprint, and that was while investigation a black magic coven in Brighton. Could there be a link at Clapham Woods?

One part of a black coven's ritual involves the burning of sulphur, which could account for the acrid smell and fumes reported in the woods. Some also practice de-materialisation of small creatures, which launches the creature's "life spark" into the area. Stringer decided to match the footprint with footprints in folklore and witchcraft, unknown to him the footprint matched that of the demon "Amduscias" as illustrated in De Plancy's "Dictionnaire infernal".

The woods have since the 1700's had strange incidents occurring, in fact the report even claimed that an acrid smell occurred, does this mean that there has been a black coven in the area since then? Also there is the disappearance of Rev. Snelling, vicar of Clapham church, one day he decided to walk back through the woods after shopping at Worthing, he has not been seen since.

Many locations around the country seem to be "gateways of strangeness" a combination of UFO, ghost and weird sightings occur within relatively small areas. I've investigated similar areas before like Byland Abbey in North Yorkshire being the focus of similar incidents. During the early 1990's a research group, investigating a spate of recent UFO reports were shocked to witness a magickal ritual occurring in a Christian centre of worship, this was after three months of intense UFO activity. As with many such places, Byland's paranormal activity dates back to the Norman times, however that is another story altogether.

JAMES DURHAM'S FIGHT WITH A GHOST

In ghost history there are many mentions of encounters of ghosts which results in violence, the most famous case is that of novelist Captain Frederick Marryat who while staying at Raynham Hall decided to 'ghost hunt'.

While walking along an upstairs hallway he encountered the Hall's infamous Brown Lady, she was carrying a lantern and glided past them through a door. Marryat noticed she was grinning at him so he leapt out and fired a pistol at her sending the bullet straight through her head, lodging in a wall.

There have been many questions about Marryat's claims, but none so on the following, equally perplexing is the following story of James Durham, a Darlington night watchman's encounter with fight with a ghost.

James Durham gave a witness statement to Rev Harry Kendal, a Congregational Minister in the late 19th century, at Darlington. The statement said that James Durham was a night-watchman at the Old Darlington and Stockton Station, dated 9th December, 1890:-

> "I was a night-watchman at the old Darlington and Stockton Railway Station, at the town of Darlington, a few yards from the first station that ever existed. I was there 15 years. I used to go on duty about 8 pm and came off at 6 am.
>
> I had been there a little while, perhaps two or three years, and at about midnight, or 12.30 am,

I was feeling rather cold standing here and there, so I said to myself, "I will go away down and get something to eat". There was a porters' room, where a fire was kept on, and a coal-house was connected to it. So I went down the steps, took off my overcoat and had just sat down on the bench opposite the fire, and turned up the gas, when a strange man came out of the coal-house, followed by a black retriever dog. As soon as he entered, my eye was upon him and his eye upon me, and we intently watched each other as he moved on to the front of the fire.

There he stood, looking at me, and a curious smile came over his countenance.

He had a stand-up collar and a cut-away coat, with gilt buttons and a Scotch cap. All at once he struck at me and I had the impression that he had hit me. I upped with my fist and struck back at him. My fist seemed to go through him and struck against the stone above the fireplace, and knocked the skin off my knuckles. The man seemed to be struck back into the fire, and uttered a strange unearthly squeak. Immediately, the dog gripped me by the calf of my leg, and seemed to cause me pain. The man recovered his position, called off the dog with a sort of a click of the tongue, and then went back into the coal-house, followed by the dog. I lighted my dark lantern and looked into the coal-house, but there was neither dog nor man, and no outlet for them except the one by which they had entered.

I was satisfied that what I had seen was ghostly, and it accounted for the fact that when the man had first come into the place where I sat, I had not challenged him. Next day, and for several weeks, my account caused quite a commotion, and a host of people spoke to me about it, among the rest, old Edward Pease, father of railways and his three sons, John, Joseph and Henry. Old Edward sent for me to his house and asked all particulars. He and others put this question to me: "are you sure that you were not asleep and had a nightmare?"

My answer was quite sure for I had not been a minute in the cellar and was just going to get something to eat. I was certainly not under the influence of strong drink, for I was then, as I have been for 49 years, a teetotaler. My mind at that time was perfectly free from trouble.

What increased the excitement was the fact that a man, a number of years before, who was employed in the office of the station, had committed suicide and was carried into this very cellar. I knew nothing of this circumstance, nor of the body of the man, but Mr Pease, and others who had known him, told me my description exactly corresponded to his appearance and the way he dressed, and also he had a black retriever just like the one that gripped me. I should add that no mark or effect remained on the spot where I seemed to be seized".

Mr Kendall made his own comments on the case:-

"Mr Durham has attended my church for 25 years and I have testimony going back that length of time to the effect that he has given the same account of the extraordinary experiences. It is a long time since he retired from the post of night-watchman, and he has since become a wealthy man. He is one of the strongest men I have ever met, able to do his 40 miles a day, walking and running with the hounds and not feel stiff the day after. I forwarded this strange narrative to Prof. Sidgwick, President of the S.P.R., who expressed a wish for fuller assurance that Mr Durham was not asleep at the time of the vision. I gave, in reply, the following four reasons for believing that he was awake:-

"Firstly, he was accustomed, as a night-watchman, to be up all night, and therefore not likely to feel sleepy from that cause. Secondly, he had scarcely been a minute in the cellar and feeling hungry was just about to get something to eat. Thirdly, if he was asleep at the beginning of the vision, he must have been awake enough during the latter part of it, when he knocked the skin off his knuckles. Fourthly, there was his own testimony, which was confident. I strongly incline to the opinion that there was objective cause for the vision, and that it was genuinely apparitional".

Mr Kendall visited the station and was taken to the porters' room, down the steps. He noted that the coalhouse was still there and also the gas bracket that Mr Durham had turned on the night in question. His guide, an old railway official, remembered the clerk, a man called John Winter, who had committed suicide, and showed Mr Kendall the place where Winter had shot himself with a pistol. In dress and appearance, Winter corresponded exactly with the phenomenon described by James Durham, and he had certainly owned a black retriever.

In October 2000, two amateur historians, Olive Howe and Irene McCloud confirmed the identity of the ghost that appeared to James Durham. During a trawl of Darlington's archives they found the death certificate of a "ticket clerk" called Thomas Munroe Winter, who committed suicide in 1845, aged 29.

In a quote to The Northern Echo the women told,

> "When we bought a copy of his death certificate we were elated to find that his cause of death was 'shot himself with a pistol, being in a state of unsound mind' and his occupation was 'ticket clerk'. We had found the ghost."

GHOST OF THE POLISH AIRMAN

The bleak peat bogs of Northern Lincolnshire not only hold prehistoric finds such as Roman Villas and Prehistoric villages, the bogs still retain the bodies of people killed in the Second World War.

In World War 2, Lindholme Prison was used as a RAF base for Wellington Bombers who took part in the first bombing raids on Berlin. On the first raid a bomber overshot the runway and crashed in to the bog, killing all five members of its Polish crew. For years afterwards, the moors were haunted by a figure in flying costume that appeared at Midnight, asking strangers directions in a foreign tongue.

The stories soon spread to the local villages of Finningley and Hatfield that the distinctive tail of the aircraft could sometimes be seen rising and sinking again when the ghost was on the prowl. In the 1950s the base was the home to a squadron of Avro Lincoln's, the ghost still appeared. One night a mechanic working late was so scared by an encounter with the ghost that he skipped duty and was brought up on a charge.

The ghost would continue to appear in the middle of night often standing beside the bed of the pilots. One pilot was so shocked by the apparition that he let out a scream that woke the whole dormitory.

In the 1970's the wreckage of the Wellington Bomber was finally recovered and the remains of four airmen were buried in a local cemetery.

In 1975, Lieutenant Colonel Stephen Jenkins and a RAF squadron leader were returning from a training course at nearby RAF Finningley when they spotted a figure dressed in flying kit, standing near the spot where the bomber crashed.

The story drew to a close in 1987 when peat workers found the forty-six year old corpse of a Polish airman. He was never identified and in November of that year he was laid to rest in a military cemetery.

Since being laid to rest the ghost has not been seen, but on cold clear winter nights, the moon casts strange shadows across those bleak bogs of Lincolnshire. If you get to drive along Lindholme Road, keep an eye out for that glimmer at the side of the road – was it a reflection or something else

OXFORD'S HAUNTED COLLEGES

Oxford, famed for its educational colleges, dreamy spires and ghosts, is one city worth venturing if looking for the unusual and architectural. Over the years I have investigated many buildings in Oxfordshire, but sadly not it's most haunted locations – it's colleges!

Magdalen College in Oxford has been the site of many types of hauntings including ghostly noises, whispering, footsteps and apparitions. The college was founded in 1458 by Bishop Waynflete, Bishop of Winchester. The original site on which it was built included the thirteen-century St John's Hospital whose buildings extended east as far as the river.

Reported in Isis magazine in 5th June 1968, one Sunday morning very early, a student who was walking across the dew-soaked college lawn towards the Colonnade arches saw with astonishment a black-clad figure moving from the cloisters towards him. He said that the figure glided rather than walked in complete silence and with no movement of the gown it wore. The student stared hard at it but where its head should have been, he saw only the wooden door twenty yards further on leading to the arches. As it came into a stronger light on reaching the entrance to the staircase it vanished.

Many more students claim to have seen the silent black figure often walking keeping pace with them as they cross the lawn. On 13th February 1987 a more terrifying apparition appeared Catriona Oliphant, at the time a twenty six year old language student.

She was sleeping late that morning when she was awakened by sounds of mysterious whisperings and then witnessing the locked door of her room opening. She then felt a strong physical "presence" moving towards her and then lean over her bed. She was too terrified to move or scream, and was only able to move when it disappeared. So great was the shock of the encounter, Catriona slept next two nights in the sick room of the college.

Two other colleges that would be worth ghost hunting, are Exeter College where the headless spectre of John Crocker haunts the site of his tomb in the chapel. The Elizabethan scholar appears dressed in a yellow jacket, gown and breeches.

St John's College's ghost dates back four hundred years. In 1645, Archbishop Laud was beheaded for his belief in the church against Parliament and was buried beneath the altar in the chapel of his college. His ghost is unconventional. In its most spectacular form, it bowls its head towards the feet of anyone unlucky enough to meet it. In a quieter mode, he walks in the normal way but a few inches off the ground, probably reflecting the way the earth has settled over the centuries.

GHOSTS OF BALGONIE CASTLE

The ghost for which Balgonie is most famous has been seen by the Laird and other members of his family, and also by visitors.

The Sibbald family built Balgonie Castle in Fife in the 14th century, with additions made to the structure over the following three centuries. The castle has been visited by both James the IV and Mary Queen of Scots and was for many years the seat of the Earls of Leven.

In January 1716 the infamous Rob Roy MacGregor paid Balgonie a visit with some 200 clansmen and 20 Hanoverian prisoners. Other famous visitors to Balgonie Castle have included Daniel Defoe, Dr Benjamin Rush (signatory of the American Declaration of Independence), James Boswell and Dr Johnson.

The 8th Earl of Leven sold Balgonie in 1824 to Sir James Balfour of Whittinghame (grandfather of A J Balfour, 1st Earl Balfour, Prime Minister 1902-05) who gave the estate to his second son Charles.

By the 1840s letters were appearing in the Edinburgh press concerning the appalling state of Balgonie. The roofs were later taken off to avoid paying Roof Tax.

Following heavy vandalism of the 1960s, the Castle was sold to David Maxwell, from Edinburgh, in 1971. He carried out restoration to the Tower before selling to the present Laird, Raymond Morris of Balgonie & Eddergoll, in 1985.

The ghost for which Balgonie is most famous has been seen by the Laird and other members of his family, and also by visitors.

Known as "Green Jeannie", she has wandered the ruinous 1702 wing for over two centuries. The Laird believes her favourite walk is between two rooms linked by a doorway. She walks in a left to right direction behind two barred windows, stopping to peer into the walled courtyard from the second window.

During an interview for Norman Adam's "Haunted Scotland" book, The Laird's wife described Jeannie, "She is pea green in colour. Her face appears to be hidden by a hood."

She saw the ghost when she let out the family's deerhounds around 2:00am.

Another ghost that frequents the castle is that of an old man. While the Laird's wife rested in an armchair in the Great Hall, she opened her eyes to find a goatee-bearded apparition "grey like a statue" - in 17th century costume staring at her.

Other ghosts include a grey man who appears to be opening non-existent doors in the courtyard, and a man's head that floats around the first floor hall!

Norman Adams mentions another sighting: "In 1996 as a waitress set the tables for a banquet...she was touched on the back. All day and night conversation could be heard, although no actual words were recognisable. Female laughter has been heard coming from the hall when empty."

The ABC Family TVshow "Scariest Places on Earth" recently held an all night vigil at the castle - with terrifying consequences! The ABC Family described the show as, "then an American couple seeking a suitable place for their wedding visits Balgonie Castle in Fife, Scotland, they soon learn that what looks like a romantic retreat from the outside is in fact a place of terror."

SCREAMING SKULLS

For thousands of years across many different cultures across the world people have believed that the head or skull has held the soul. Some tribes would preserve the skulls of their fallen enemies and the Celts would decorate their shrines with skulls.

In Britain we have a strange folklore of skulls that scream if taken from the location that they are held.

At Wardley Hall in Lancashire the skull of 16th century Catholic martyr Father Ambrose Barlow is on view at the head of the staircase with the legend that if anybody removes it the skull will emit a blood-curdling scream!

Burton Agnes Hall in Yorkshire has another screaming skull legend, this one belonging to Anne Griffiths. After being attacked and beaten by robbers, Anne in her dying breaths expressed the wish that her head should be buried in the home that she so much loved. Nevertheless her family buried her in the village churchyard.

After the funeral, terrifying groans and poltergeist activity such as doors slamming and crashes were heard around the house. The dead girl's body was exhumed and her skull was exhumed and bricked up in a wall off the staircase. Although in recent times the skull has been on display without any side effects.

Bettiscombe Manor in Dorset probably has the most famous screaming skull legend in Britain. In the 18th Century, a member of the Pinney family returned from living in the West Indies and returned with a black slave. Shortly after returning the slave died after making his master swear that he would be buried in his homeland. The Squire broke his promise and the slave was buried in the local churchyard.

Similar to that of the Burton Agnes Skull, the skull of the slave began to make agonising screams that so much disturbed passers by that they asked the Squire to make amense. Since then the skull has remained on show at Bettiscombe Manor.

As with many legends the truth is often very different from the legend. Analysis during the 1960's confirmed that the skull was in fact two thousand years old and was that of a girl. The legend remains intact that if the skull is ever removed from the manor the person who moves it will die within a year.

The power of the death's head certainly dates back to pre-history and when our ancestors believed that the skull contained the soul but also the skull is very important in magic.

In Papua, widows would impale their dead husband's skulls on poles to ward away spirits and unwanted attention. In England the trail of the witch Anne Chattox, head of a family of Lancashire Witches was accused of digging up three skulls from a churchyard to use in some ritual or demonic recipe. For this she was hanged.

The Celts often took the heads of enemies killed in battle, and kept these both as trophies and as offerings to the gods. The great stone shrine at Roquepertuse had skull-niches in the wall, some filled with representations of heads and others filled with actual skulls.

Throughout the years the skull has been seen as a mascot, trophy or charm and this is represented within the screaming skulls legends that still linger on, in England today.

THE JORROCK'S SKULL

Our next destination is "Jorrocks", a Derby pub that was originally one of the city's most well-known coaching inns when it was known as "The George." It was originally built in 1648 and is the home to some of the strangest stories in Derby.

In 1992, during building work in the cellar, a skull, which seemed to have marks of violence on it, was unearthed four feet below the cellar floor. The police were called in and the skull was sent to Nottingham for forensic examination. Was a huge murder hunt about to be launched? Would the pub have to close while the police made enquiries? The results of the forensic examination were eagerly anticipated.

However, it was all something of an anti-climax when the skull was dated at approximately 917 A.D. and returned to the landlord. If there had been a murder then the perpetrator was long since dust. The skull was believed to be that of a woman – no, not because the jaw was open! As it happens the lower jaw is missing. The likely explanation for it being there is that when the "George" was built it was still the custom to bury in the foundations a skull, a pair of shoes and a dead cat to ward off witches and evil spirits. Some leather remains and animal bones were found at the same time. So the damage to the skull was probably caused when it was buried. Instead of being re-interred in the cellar, it is now kept on a high shelf behind the bar.

Ever since the skull was exhumed, the witches and evil spirits seem to be having a field day on the premises. Reports say that crockery has been moved but remains unbroken, objects have been thrown at members of staff, and groans have been heard down in the cellar. Even more bizarrely, glasses have been known to shatter usually in female customers' hands – but at least the poltergeist has the decency to wait until they are empty.

The other activity in the building is believed to be linked to the "Derby Blues". In September, 1745 the Duke of Devonshire was charged with the task of protecting Derby from the Jacobites. Following a meeting with local dignitaries at the inn, it was agreed that a regiment of volunteers be raised. The regiment was to be lead by the Duke's eldest son, the Marquess of Harrington.

The "Blues", paraded on 3rd December, but they were completely untrained. Within hours news arrived that the Jacobite army of between 5,500 and 7,800 men had reached Ashbourne and was heading for Derby.

By the time the first of the invading army entered Derby, the "Blues" had withdrawn "in some disarray" to Nottingham. By the following day, they had withdrawn even further - to Mansfield – much to the amusement of the enemy. The "Blues" had been followed out of Derby by most of the city's dignitaries and Bonnie Prince Charlie was proclaimed King. But, by 6th December, the Jacobite rebellion was all but over as Charles was persuaded to retreat to Scotland.

However, the Duke's reputation never really recovered from the ridiculous affair of the "Blues".

The figure of a man with long hair and wearing a long blue coat has often been seen walking along the landing in the middle of the night. He then descends the stairs and disappears in the bar area. Is he re-enacting the shame of the "Blues" ignominious retreat? Does he still disappear in shame after all this time – or is he looking for somewhere to hide? A similar figure has also been seen in the area of the ladies' toilets – is he looking for safety in there? But perhaps we are doing this lone soldier an injustice. Could he be the only one of the "Blues" to remain and face the enemy?

ROYALIST DEVIL OF WOODSTOCK MANOR

Woodstock Manor was once home that for hundreds of years was graced by many Kings and Queen's of England. King Henry I kept leopards and porcupines here, and the future Elizabeth I was a prisoner in the lodge, if the Manor still stood, its rich history and architecture would have made it a national treasure. Sadly in the 1720 the manor was demolished and all what remains is a stone pillar on the Glyme Valley Way.

From Woodstock Manor comes the tale of the "Royalist Devil of Woodstock", whether the spirit was the devil or an ingenious follower of the King, it disturbed the Parliamentarians so much, they refused to occupy the building again.

Formerly Woodstock Palace, Woodstock Manor was visited by Cromwell's commissioners on 13th October 1649, with order to remove all evidence of the King's occupancy there. During their stay they were victims of sever poltergeist activity, believed at the time to be the disembodied spirit of a Royalist.

Three days after their arrival at the Manor House, paranormal activity began. Two of the commissioners, and members of their staff, saw a phantom dog entering the room they were using as a bedroom. It went over to their beds and started gnawing at the cords.

The next night was even more eventful, their beds were hoisted up and down so violently by invisible hands that they were said to be a mass of bruises the following morning. The wood from the King's Oak, which by then had been cut into small pieces, was found scattered around the dining room, and furniture was found overturned. Objects were hurled about various rooms and candles were blown out as soon as they were lighted. Bedclothes were flung from their beds.

On 29th October, the walls were shaken and the windows broken by loud noises that were heard all over the neighbourhood and the servants were panic-stricken. One of the servants was nearly killed by another, when he appeared during the night dressed only in his shirt, and was mistaken for a ghost.

For the next few nights there was complete silence but on the 2nd November the sounds were heard again, this time seeming to come from three different places at the same time. The noise became that bad that it scared away local poachers who were wandering in the grounds, leaving their poaching equipment where it lay as they fled. One of the commissioners saw a hoof, as it was about to kick out the flame of his candle. Drawing his sword to strike the "beast", invisible hands knocked the weapon from his grasp, and then knocked him out with a single blow.

After that incident, the commissioners decided to give up their task and left Woodstock, declaring that "all the fiends of hell had been let loose on them". No more was heard of the poltergeist, although the Puritans always avoided the Manor House after that and it was considered haunted for the remaining days of the Commonwealth.

THE BRINKLOW HILL MYSTERIES

With its tales of hauntings, UFO activity and alleged satanic murder, Brinklow Hill, Leicestershire is one of the mysterious sites in Britain.

The Warwickshire town of Brinklow has a notable topographical feature – an imposing grassy mound known locally as the Tump. Built on a natural rise, and offering a striking view of the surrounding countryside, the hill and its nearby earthworks represent one of the best preserved motte-and-bailey castle sites in the country. However, the name of Brinklow itself suggests a much older settled community, or at least a site that was important to people long before the Norman Conquest.

The name is thought to originate from two Old English elements: the personal name Brynca, and the word hlaw, meaning "hill" in the sense of tumulus or burial mound. This ancient derivation implies that there was almost certainly a man-made "tump" here long before the Normans exploited the site to build their castle.

The mound was already at least five hundred years old when the Normans decided to build upon it. The Fosse Way, which is Roman road running two hundred miles from Exeter to Lincoln, deviates in its straight course here and only here to go around the mound.

To date, the mound at Brinklow remains unexcavated, so it is not known for certain whether it is the final resting place of some minor British chieftain, circumvented by the Romans, or later owned by an Anglo-Saxon called Brynca, even perhaps the grave of Brynca himself. What does seem certain is that there was some form of settlement or human activity long before the Normans built their castle or later their fine church dedicated to St. John the Baptist.

The Legend
The following is a brief introduction to the mysteries that were promoted by Graham Philips, a "historical detective" and one time psychic quester. During the early 1980s and 1990s he wrote a series of books (along with author and researcher Andrew Collins) about 'psychic quests' in the Midlands of England.

The books began with "The Green Stone" – about the finding of the Meon Stone and its relation to a possible occult death on Meon Hill. Soon followed "Eye of Fire" centred around the strange activity around Brinklow Hill and a character called John Lang.

Graham's own website claims "In The Eye of Fire Graham Phillips and Martin Keatman investigate claims of the macabre haunting of Brinklow Hill... Many witnesses tell of seeing a sinister dark figure in Victorian clothes standing on top of the hill. However, the Brinklow case is more than just a run-of-the-mill haunting. Strange electrical anomalies occur in the area at the time the ghost is seen. Back in 1982, one night when dozens of local people claimed to have seen the ghost standing ominously on Brinklow Hill, the hill was hit by multiple lightning strikes that blasted apart three trees that had stood on top for decades."

In a further article Graham also claims "For over a century the ghost was said to haunt both Brinklow Hill and the Raven Inn that stands just below it. Not only was the ghost of a dark Victorian figure said to have been seen in the bar, but frightening poltergeist activity was reported by both the landlords and patrons alike. The ghost was even claimed to have been caught on film when a group of researchers photographed Brinklow Hill.

My Researches

After reading The Green Stone and the other related books I began to look into my own research in the area. During the early 1990's I often studied Earth Mysteries and Leys in Warwickshire and Leicestershire, not knowing of Philip's publication or supposed incidents.

Back tracking through my researches and reassessing the case, I can provide what could be additional information that could back up Philip's theories and ideas. Firstly I decided to analyse old ordnance survey maps of the area to see if there were any further clues to the origins of the paranormal activity.

Sun Worship at Brinklow

By road the Tump is approached by Ell Lane, which could hint at sun worship. The name "Ell" links with the Greek "ele" meaning "refulgent" or "Torch/A Bright one". Ele also obviously links with Helios, the Greek god of the Sun.

The reverence of the sun as a god came from the east to Greece where he was a popular god, in fact the

Colossus of Rhodes was in his honour. People sacrificed oxen, rams, goats, and white horses to Helios.

The Cabalists (one of the oldest and most influential subgroups in the whole Order of Hermes) also understood "Ell" to mean "the most Luminous".

It certainly seemed interesting that an ancient pathway next the Tump could insinuate Sun worship, but could there be other clues?

At first I didn't notice it but it was there in front of me all the time – St John the Baptist's church. The church was built in 1215, it was an early Norman church although extensively altered in the late 18th century. It dedication to St John the Baptist is a further clue to possible sun worship.

St John the Baptist is a midsummer solar saint, his feast day usually given to hill top churches associated with pre-Christian solar deities. During the summer solstice these sites were known to burn bonfires, even today, people in East Europe still mark Midsummer's Eve with festivals or dances and bonfires that light up the night sky.

I decided to look at the name Brinklow Hill again and to see if there could be any clues in the name itself. When checking the name Brynca, I noticed that in Welsh the name Bryn also means " mount that is a large hill" and that Low mean "valley". Further more, if we stay with the welsh translation, Haul is welsh for Sun. So if we look at the name again in Welsh we have the name "Sun Hill over the Valley". Could this be the right translation or just conjecture?

I also looked at the names of the public houses in Brinklow and both have interesting names. "The White Lion" is one name that has instantly links to the sun – the Lion is a solar symbol, Christ's resurrection is often symbolised by the Lion as well. "The Raven", links to Bad News, a Bad Omen. The Mithraic cults would sacrifice the Raven for being the messenger of the gods.

Another possible clue comes from Graham Philip's whose investigation of Brinklow Hill included a possible bizarre ritual murder.

Langley Connection
It is alleged that in 1865 a serving girl named Sarah Haynes was found strangled on Brinklow Hill. A self-proclaimed Satanist named John Newton Langley and a member of an occult society that met in the grounds of nearby Coombe Abbey fell under suspicion for the murder. Philips further alleges, "sometime later Langley himself disappeared and both the murder and his disappearance remained unsolved"

If John Langley was an alleged Satanist working in the area at the time, could it be that he too noticed the connection between Brinklow Hill and the Solar Worship? In magical tradition, Lucifer (meaning "light-bringer") was the sun god and brother of Diana, the moon goddess (Not to be confused with the Christian

"Lucifer", also known as Satan). It would be interesting to find out if Sarah Haynes was murdered near or on the Mid-Summer Solstice.

A Psychic Quest
Again I must tell you that I have not read the Eye of Fire, but looking at my correspondences back in 1990, I was able to find a report of a psychic quest at Brinklow Hill undertaken by Rita Goold (a physical medium) and Clive Potter, who is still a UFO researcher and psychic quester.

"On Sunday September 17th 1989, four people met up at Brinklow, one of the party, Rita Goold had received psychic suggestions that something of interest was buried on the hill.

Using dowsing rods two 6" daggers (or paper knives) were located, buried either side of a stile that forms one of the entrances to the site. After a heavy down pour the team decided to leave the hill and drive back to Leicester with Rita.

As they drove Clive noticed that in the back of the car, the dowsing rods appeared to be moving and jumping more than would be expected from the surface of the road. At that moment Rita alerted Clive to a mysterious light above the trees to the left of the road.

The light was white and the size of a pea at arm's length, it did not hurt the eyes to look at and the light now seemed to be travelling in the centre of the road. It then descended in a feathery motion causing them to brake. The light was stationary for a second so Rita began to reverse her car, concerned for the safety of her car.

The light moved towards them for about ten seconds then moved from the right and hit the road about five car lengths in front of them. The light then increased speed and caused a "whooshing" sound as it passed and rocked the car. The white light continued to hit the road. They turned round to watch the light as it disappeared round a bend in the road.

The two witnesses contacted Mike Rowe of the Ball Lightning Division of Storm and Tornado Research Organisation who reported that the only lightning reported was in the extreme north-west of Scotland, and that was eighteen hours earlier. Both witnesses were convinced that the phenomena experienced was related to the successful psychic quest for the daggers."

The Brinklow Ley
Stretching across Warwickshire there are a series of leys and one of them runs through Brinklow. The Brinklow Ley begins at Coombe Abbey where Graham Philips alleges that John Langley used to meet an occult society. In the grounds of the abbey is a small and inconspicuous mound, 40ft in diameter and 3 feet high, there is a possibility it could be a recent mound, however Coombe Abbey did replace an earlier settlement.

The ley then continues along the Fossway through Brinklow Hill and then on to the Easenhall Church and then a nearby Earthworks.

The ley continues to Cotton House, a mound and possibly a late eighteenth century folly. The Brinklow Ley is an east-west alignment and with at least two churches associated with it. I do believe that further investigation does need to take place to further validate it.

A Semi-Conclusion
Over the years I have interviewed many Brinklow residents about the hill and its unusual atmosphere, indeed some residents have been witnesses to some very strange paranormal activity. Its seems that the phenomena that was discussed over twenty years ago still continues today even if Graham Philips believes that he may have rid the Hill of its hauntings. Why not venture to Brinklow Hill and its haunted pub, "The Raven", and try to experience something weird?

THE ISLE OF THE DEAD

Glastonbury or Avalon? Glastonbury was both an Isle of the Dead and an Isle of the Blessed. Two pagan deities are known to reside here and both are related to the underworld.

The fairy king Avalloch is said to have presided over the town, little is known about him although it's believed he was the father of the Mother Goddess Modron. He used the Tor as a gateway where the souls of the dead can pass freely. Another deity also associated with the Tor, Gwynn ap Nudd of the Welsh tradition used the Tor for a doorway to the dead. Gwynn was the Lord of the Underworld and the Wild Hunt, it was believed on dark nights when the moon is full that you could hear his ghost hounds traversing the sky hunting for souls.

These traditions must have built up around Glastonbury for a reason, I believe that since the dawn of man, the Tor and Glastonbury has been a site of burial and ultimately rebirth.

Glastonbury Abbey
Many legends are attached to the Abbey, many believe that the Holy Thorn tree that can be seen in the grounds originated from Joseph of Arimathea's staff. Others are convinced that King Arthur and Queen Guinevere are buried in the Abbey grounds. Whatever one believes, the Abbey was one of the richest and most elaborate in the country and can celebrate over two thousand years years of Christianity.

Some proclaim that King Arthur was laid to rest here after the battle of Badon Hill, some people believe this was a site near Cadbury Castle. Arthur was brought to Avalon and laid to rest in the centre of the abbey. Most legends state that Arthur lays in an eternal sleep until England needs such a hero again, at Glastonbury the legend is quite the reverse.

Local legends claim that after Arthur's death a powerful negative spirit, a black armoured knight with glowing red eyes and a burning desire to eradicate all records of the ancient Arthurian legends began to appear in the Abbey grounds. In the past and even more recently a number of researchers have witnessed this figure in the Abbey grounds, nobody knows why he is trying to destroy the memory of Arthur but the legend is now over four hundred years old.

During the 1970's the Ghost Club investigated the Lady's Chapel. One investigator walked into the Chapel and was aware of a white-robed figure ahead of him. Thinking he was witnessing a ceremony of some sort he walked quickly to the centre of the chapel and saw a column of figures all walking towards the exit. He couldn't determine whether they were nuns or monks just that they where dressed in white habits. He started to make his way out of the Abbey when he began to feel strange, he believed he was caught up in a vortex, he began to lose sight of the figures and everything was back to normal.

The Tribunal

Situated on Glastonbury's High Street, the Tribunal is a spot of great significance, unknown to the tourist, little known to, and less realised by the inhabitants. This is the Tribunal Building, where the Chief Abbot formerly dispensed justice. The Tribunal, is a beautiful building with lovely ceilings and a repose of its own, is now the tourist information centre and museum. However the Ghosts here are seen not just above ground but also below.

During the 1960's a gas worker had to explore the tunnels for the latest gas pipes to be laid. He entered the tunnel at the Tribunal and ventured below. He lit his lantern and began to walk down the tunnel examining the structure. Suddenly he realised that there was somebody ahead of him but carrying a lamp with a candle. He believed it was a colleague of his who must have entered the tunnel from the other side. He began to shout and walk towards him but there was no response from the colleague.

He stopped and began to wave his lamp side to side to cause a distraction, the lamp copied the movements. He once again shouted his colleague's name but once again there was no reply. He stood watching the lamp as it started to dim and then fade away. He returned back upstairs where he found his colleague sat waiting for him. He realised his colleague wasn't the person with the lamp, but not only that, but the tunnel was blocked off at the other side in the early 1900's.

The George and Pilgrims
This article on Glastonbury's hauntings wouldn't be complete without The George and Pilgrims hotel.

The George and Pilgrims was built in the 15th Century to accommodate pilgrims visiting the Abbey. There are many ghosts attached to the building and its one of the most haunted hotels in Somerset, if not the country.

In the oldest bedrooms most of the ghost stories are found. They fall into the nighttime visitor category. One nightly ghost is that of a fat and cheerful monk, he is often seen walking through on wall to the next, laughing as he does so. One night one visitor actually felt the monk bump into the bed shaking her awake.

When researching the ghost story its believed the monk had quite a sad ending. For whatever reason the monk committed suicide in the room now known as the haunted cell. However, it seems that he is not bitter, in fact the opposite, for people feel happiness and delight when he is around.

Recently a travel journalist with the guardian visited the George and Pilgrims to write a report about Glastonbury. During the night his wife woke up and saw at the bottom of her bed a tall gentleman with long arms looking at her. She crossed herself and decided to reach out and touch him – her hands passed right through him. She screamed awakening her husband.

Another ghost is one that manifests itself in sounds and smells. Staff have often heard in the function arguments and the smell of cigar smoke coming from the room, when they have opened the door, all that is left is the remnants of smoke in the air.

There are countless other tales from this spiritual town that could fill many pages but I leave it to you to explore Glastonbury's darker side.

THE PHANTOM HAND

Now a classic haunting from a very trustworthy person, the following account is from the Rev. D. W. G. Gwynne who was a physician in Holy Orders.

In 1853 he lived with his wife at an unnamed house near Taunton. Both he and his wife were made uncomfortable by auditory experiences to which they could find no clue.

He proceeds, "I now come to the mutual experience of something that is as fresh in its impression as if it were the occurrence of yesterday. During the night I became aware of a draped figure passing across the foot of the bed towards the fire-place. I had the impression that the arm was raised, pointing with the hand towards the mantel-piece, on which a night light was burning. Mrs. Gwynne at this moment seized my arm, and the light was extinguished. Notwithstanding, I distinctly saw the figure returning towards the door, and being under the impression that one of our servants had found her way into our room, I leapt out of bed to intercept the intruder, but found, and saw, nothing. I rushed to the door, and endeavoured to follow the supposed intruder, and it was not until I found the door locked, as usual, that I was painfully impressed. I need hardly say that Mrs. Gwynne was in a very nervous state. She asked me what I had seen, and I told her. She had seen the same figure, but her impression was that the figure placed its hand over the night-light and extinguished it.

"The night-light in question was relit and placed in a toilette basin, and burned naturally. I tried to convince myself that it might have been a gust of wind down the chimney that put the light out ; but that will not account for the spectral appearance, which remains a mystery.

Mrs Gwynne wrote to the authors of "Phantasms of the living", a classic book by three leading members of Society for Psychical Research.

Mrs. Gwynne wrote, "In addition to my husband's statement, which I read, I can only say that the account he has given you accords with my remembrance of the unearthly vision,' but I distinctly saw the hand of the phantom placed over the night-light, which was at once extinguished. I tried to cling to Dr. Gwynne, but he leapt out of bed with a view, as he afterwards said, of intercepting some supposed intruder. The door was locked as usual, and was so when he tried it. He lit a candle at once, and looked under the bed, and into a closet, but saw nothing. The night-light was also relit, which was placed on the wash-stand, and together with the candle, remained burning all night. I must observe that I had never taken to use night-lights before we lived there, and only did so when I had been so often disturbed and alarmed by sighs and heavy breathing close to my side of the bed. Dr. Gwynne, on the appearance of the phantom, in order to calm my agitated state, tried to reason with me, and to persuade me that it might have been the effects of the moonlight and clouds passing over the openings of the shutter, and possibly that a gust of wind might have extinguished the light, but I knew differently. When we had both been awakened at the same moment apparently, and together saw that unpleasant figure, tall and as it were draped like a nun, deliberately walk up to the mantel-piece and put out the light with the right hand, there could be no mistake about it ; and I distinctly heard the rustling sound of garments as the figure turned and left through the door, after my husband's attempt to stop it with his open arms. The moonlight was very clear and the white dimity curtains only partly closed."

SCOTLAND'S MOST HAUNTED ROAD

The stretch of the A75 from Annan to Gretna Green is claimed to be the most haunted road in Scotland and with plans to improve it, local residents believe it will unleash angry spirits.

Hundreds of weird sightings and unexplained accidents have been reported in the area over the past fifty years. The fifteen mile stretch of the A75 from Annan in Dumfriesshire to Gretna Green is claimed to be the most haunted road in Scotland and the Scottish Office plans to improve it but the local residents believe that it will unleash the already angry spirits.

Donna Maxwell from New Path, Annan reported "It was in July when I was driving back from my mother's house in Eastriggs around 10:00pm on a clear, well-lit night...All of a sudden a man appeared in front of my car and just stood there, looking sad. I was doing around 50mph and I slammed on the brakes. I was convinced I hit him but I couldn't see anyone so I drove to Annan police station."

"The police went out and searched for a body but found nothing. I couldn't understand it. Since then I have heard other people talking about seeing the same man standing in the road just looking at the cars. Maybe he is searching for some one. I don't regard myself as someone who believes in the paranormal but after that I have changed my mind. I still can't go down that road at night, I take the bypass instead."

Police sergeant Graham Young was so concerned he even put out a description of the man who was in his late 30's, wearing a red jumper and dark trousers. He said "I have an open mind about this incident. I was born and raised in this area so I know all about the ghosts in this town. Mrs Maxwell was convinced she had hit someone so we treated it like any other road traffic accident."

A resident of Dornock, a hamlet the road passes through, said "Some people might think we are being stupid but I have lived here eight years and I have seen and heard a lot of strange things..we don't want anything done that might disrupt the spirits that live here. I'm too terrified to go down that road at night just now and I dread to think what will happen if they dig it up."

One of the spooks has been seen on two occasions – forty-five years apart.

Margaret Ching reported her frightening encounter with an old lady in a cloud of mist. The apparition was exactly as it had been described by local, Jim Carlyle when he was a lad.

Mrs Ching, from the West Midlands was being driven to Gretna by her fiancé John on the eve of their wedding there. She said "We were approaching Dornock when a kind of mist suddenly appeared and in the middle was a very old woman dressed in Victorian clothes. I couldn't see her face but I gave a yell because I thought John would hit her but the car went right through her and as it did we felt a cold shiver. We looked back and she was gone. It was a clear night with no fog or mist. I was very shaken and had to sit for a while before we could drive on."

Jim Carlyle told how the same apparition scared him twenty six years ago at the same spot. He said "I was just a lad and was going along with my girlfriend in the car when this old lady appeared in the mist, I slammed on my brakes but we went right through her."

Nearby Comlongon Castle near Dornock has its equal share of ghosts too. Owners Peter and Wendy Ptomley said "Guests have seen a white figure in a room where a lady was imprisoned years ago."

Another of the most frightening sightings happened to a Dornock woman who noticed an old man leaning against the wall. When the old man turned round he had no eyes, only black holes. When she told someone in the village, she just said "Oh you've seen him too."

THE GHOST TOWN

The small country town of Oundle in Northamptonshire, with its ancient buildings, intriguing alleyways, ancient inns and one of the finest churches in the Midlands is so satisfying to look at. Its when you delve deeper you uncover its haunted heritage..

The imposing Talbot Hotel is haunted by the sound of a woman crying at night. The Talbot stands on ancient monastic lands, and parts of the building have gothic influenced architecture. As a hotel, it offers you the chance to experience multiple ghosts.

The crying lady is believed to appear in a long white dress and stand at the top of the stairs or by the window of the conference room opposite. The staircase and windows where the ghost appears were brought here from Fotheringhay Castle when it was demolished. It is assumed that the ghost is that of Mary, Queen of Scots who, while standing at the top of these stairs received the news that she would be executed the following day.

On one occasion a guest staying in the next room heard the sound of a woman sobbing bitterly from room No.5, yet the room was empty at the time. The date was the anniversary of Mary's death.

Mary has been seen walking down the upper flight of the staircase and has also been witnessed standing near the reception counter. She has also been seen looking down into the yard from a window on the landing and is easily recognisable by her white blouse and white cap, yet she can only be seen by men.

Drumming Well Yard is the passageway that leads from the main street to the rear of the hotel. It takes its name from the well that was once located here, which warned of impending natural disasters by emitting loud drumming noises. Thus it predicted the Fire of London and the deaths of King Charles II and Oliver Cromwell, as well as other events up to the late 18th century.

Nearby Nene Cottage was once an inn, this beautiful 17th century cottage was restored to a home in the 1970's and it is the restoration that caused the new owners to be alarmed since it seemed to have awoken a ghost!

They experienced the rattling of door-handles, particularly in the late afternoon. The spare bedroom was also found to have a rather unusual atmosphere. When new owners took over the manifestations became more frequent and shadows were seen on the walls of the affected bedroom together with footsteps that were heard at night.

There have been two reported apparitions at the cottage. One is of a young girl with long black hair, seen crouching near an outhouse, wearing what looks like a nightdress. The other is of a young boy with long fair hair, wearing early 20th century-style clothes, who has been seen leaping around the garden before disappearing through the garden wall.

Dating from the seventeenth century, The Ship Inn, has a ghost who's origins date from more recent times. Seen many times by previous licensees and guests, it is believed that the ghost is a former landlord who committed suicide by throwing himself from the window of a bedroom at the front of the pub. Strangely the height from window to pavement is only seven feet – so maybe he landed unfortunately?

TIME SLIPS

An author witnesses a scene from over four hundred years ago and an off-duty policemen relives 1950's Liverpool. Do people really slip through time as easy as entering a room?

"Ghosts" are a multi-faceted phenomenon that deserves to be classified as a range of different events. Many ghost sightings are readily explained as individuals who appear out of their normal location or time; often the ghost also seems to change the surroundings of the witness, giving the impression of a "time slip".

What is open to question is whether these are glimpses into another time or does the witness or ghost does actually travel time?

Ghost hunter and author, Joan Forman collected many reports time slips from around the UK. One example concerns a Warder who was on duty in the Byward Tower, at the main entrance to the Tower of London. One night, he looked up to see five or six Beefeaters from a much earlier time, seated round a log fire, smoking pipes. Not only that, the whole room had altered in appearance. The room reverted back to its original state when the warder left the room and returned moments later. Forman gathered such an amount of evidence she was able to publish "Masks of Time" a book dedicated to this phenomena.

Forman's interest in Time Slips took her to Haddon Hall in Derbyshire, where she was to have a Time Slip of her own and allow her to develop the theory of the 'trigger factor'.

Joan entered the courtyard of Haddon Hall, pausing to admire the architecture. Without warning she 'saw' a group of four children playing at the top of the stairs, a girl about nine years old caught the attention of Joan. She had shoulder-length blonde hair, a white Dutch hat and a long green-grey silk dress with a white collar. Joan watched with in fascination the children playing in the yard "fully aware that she was not seeing with the physical eye, yet conscious of watching real action.

Joan decided to find the identity of the oldest child and entered the Hall looking at every family portrait. In the middle of the ancestral paintings, a picture of the girl she had seen was hung; it was Lady Grace Manners who died in the 1640's.

The trigger factor occurs when one is interested in their surroundings but not concentrating on them; a slip occurs at a precise place and moment and the witness is thrust seemingly, into another time.

At Leeds Castle in Kent, Alice Pollock experienced what could be called a 'classic' time slip. Alice was experimenting in the Henry VIII's rooms by touching objects in an attempt to experience events from another time. After a period of receiving no impressions whatsoever, the room suddenly changed. The room lost its modern, comfortable appearance to become cold and bare. The carpet had disappeared and there were now logs burning on the fire. A tall woman in a white dress was walking up and down the room; her face seemed in deep concentration. Not long after the room returned to its original state.

By researching in history it's was found that the rooms had been the prison of Queen Joan of Navarre, Henry V\'s stepmother and had been accused of witchcraft by her husband.

With a wealth of information available on time slips in books and the internet, many of the cases quoted are often quite old and occurred at least thirty years ago. Once case that has recently come to public attention is that of an off duty policeman.

In July 1996, in Liverpool's Bold Street, an off duty Merseyside Policeman inadvertently travelled back in time. While shopping with his wife in the city centre, one Saturday afternoon, Frank and his wife split up to buy from different shops, Carol his wife went to Dillon's Bookshop, while Frank went to a local record store.

A small 1950's box van crossed in front of Frank, honking his horn in its progress. The van's livery stated it was from 'Caplan's'. He looked down to his feet, and realised he was stood in the middle of the road. Frank crossed the road and saw that 'Dillon's Book Store' now had 'Cripps' over its entrances and moreover, the shop was selling women's handbags and shoes rather than books.

Looking around the street, Frank realised that the people he could see were dressed in the fashions from the 1940's but strangely a young woman in her 20's walked past him with a popular brand named handbag. This reassured him that he was partially in 1996; he smiled at the girl as she walked past and entered 'Cripps'.

As he followed her into the store, the interior of the building changed in a flash to that of Dillon's Bookshop in 1996. Frank questioned the young woman who had entered with him into 'Cripps', she confirmed that she too thought the shop was a clothes shop rather than a bookshop.

It has been recently proved that 'Cripps' and 'Caplan's' were actual businesses based in Liverpool during the 1950's, whether they were based in the locations specified in the story has not been confirmed.

Frank's sighting offers numerous questions, if indeed it is true. Did the box van driver see Frank as a ghost something wearing strange clothing while standing in the middle of the street? Did other shopper's see him acting 'strange' outside the 'Cripps' store in the 1950's? If he did appear, we have no record of anybody reporting such a sighting, which is a shame considering the implications if there were witnesses.

Time Slips can occur on two different levels, one being the possible reincarnation of that person, who recognises the surroundings they are visiting in this life. Another is when the slip is triggered by the witness, whether they blank their mind at a precise moment and the slip occurs, or the witness touches something that holds the memory of a previous time. Time Slips seem to have happened for many years, and viewing Frank's story they will continue for many more.

THE HAUNTED HANDS

Many roads in Devon are haunted, by a phantom either visible or audible to some. Often there is a vague atmosphere of tragedy or evil.

One road, Carter's Road, from Moretonhampsted to Princetown certainly has a haunted history incorporating the story of the "Haunted Hands".

Ghost Horse and Rider
The tale of a man walking back from Chagford to Princetown sends a slow chill down the back. The lane lies between hedges set high on walls hiding what lies beyond. The man suddenly heard a horse galloping towards him down the lane. He had no light and he could only flatten himself against the hedge and hope the horse would not hit him. There also seemed to be a rider, because he could hear the squeak of the harness. The sounds now came from the back of him, then he realised that he had not seen anything or actually heard it pass him.

There is no doubt that the road and the area surrounding it are haunted by something pretty resentful of modern intruders. For many years there have been unexplained events where people, especially travellers have reported seeing or feeling a pair of huge hairy hands.

Fatal Encounters
The "entity" seems to confine its attacks to motorcyclists. There have been at least two fatal

accidents, one, a man riding alone was thrown off his machine and killed. In the second case the rider killed, but a pillion passenger escaped with serious injuries. "I saw a hairy hand touch the handle-bar of the cycle and upset it" said the witness.

The prison doctor at Princetown was killed on the same spot in 1921. Mrs E Battiscombe, the widow of his successor wrote to author Theo Brown in 1961.

"The prison doctor (Dr Helby) was asked to go to Postbridge to attend the inquest on French (who had been thrown from his trap and killed, but on another road). He had a motorcycle and sidecar and took with him two little girls for the ride. They were the daughters of the Deputy Governor. Going down the hill in to Postbridge he was flung off the bicycle and his neck broken. There was no apparent damage to his machine. The children were thrown out on the verge and shaken but not much hurt. Villagers took charge of them and saw them home."

Another incident was recalled by Mrs Battiscombe:

"A young man undertook to run in to Princetown on his motorcycle to get something for his landlady. In about an hour he returned to Penlee, very white and shaken, and saying he had had a curious experience. He said that he had felt his hands gripped by two rough and hairy hands and every made to throw him off his machine."

In 1923 one local wrote the following story:

"It was a cold moonlit night and I was in my bunk in a caravan facing a small window at the end, under which my husband lay deeply asleep in his bunk. I awoke suddenly with a feeling of fear and danger, and quite wide-awake. I knew there was some power very seriously menacing, near us and I must act swiftly. As I at last looked up to the little window I saw something moving and as I stared, my heart beating fast, I saw it was the fingers and palm of a very large hand with many hairs on the joints and back of it, clawing up and up to the top of the window which was a little open. I knew it wished to do harm to my husband sleeping below.

Being a Christian I made the sign of the cross and I prayed very much, at once the hand slowly sank down out of sight and I knew the danger had gone."

Haunted Hands sightings are very seldom but incidents have been recorded. Manifestations have occurred in Southern Brittany and some Scottish Legends portray Hairy Hands in their stories. In the 1970's a lorry driver reported a single hand flashing across his windscreen. Partial apparitions occur commonly footsteps, floating heads and even eyes, but hands are not so frequent.

A HAUNTING VILLAGE

Most haunted village in East Anglia - tough one but I would suggest Coggeshall in Essex. There have been quite a few sightings of ghosts and it has quite a few mysteries attached to it.

There is one particular ghost present in the White Hart hotel, no-one can distinguish whether it is male or female or the history behind it. The ghost has been seen wandering the old parts of the hotel and in particular the guests lounge which is the oldest room in the hotel.

Coggeshall Curse
Fables about the mid-Essex village of Coggeshall make it one of the most intriguing in East Anglia.

The area is famed for its bizarre and obscure past. A tourist information leaflet teases curious visitors with the statement "discover sleepy unspoilt Coggeshall, where the ley lines cross and mysterious things happen."

It is rumoured that ley lines - powerful beams of energy linked to the earth's magnetic pull - actually cross in Coggeshall, creating friction.

Peter Healey, author of the Coggeshall curse, says a coven used to meet at Marks Hall and take part in bizarre rituals involving young women tied to trees. His book is packed full of weird and incredible tales about the area, including the suggestion that the warrior queen Boudica (Boadicea) is buried with her chariot and jewels in the parish.

East Street in the town used to be known as Gallows Street and St Peter's road was once known as Dead Lane. It was also thought that a set of gallows used to be situated at the Tollgate crossroads for public hangings.

Coggeshall's eerie past has also attracted ghost busters from across the country and some history books suggest a local woman was tortured by witchcraft in the 17th century.

Mr Haines said: "The town is very proud of its history. We are still uncovering hidden treasures and that is what makes the area so fascinating."

Cradle House
Cradle House was once a haven for monks who held meetings in secret rooms within the building; it is believed that these figures sometimes return to dance in the garden.

Robin's Ghost
Coggeshall is haunted by the ghost of a 16th century woodcutter named Robin, who is said to have carved a beautiful image called the 'Angel of the Christmas Mysteries' The statue was hidden during the Reformation and never found afterwards. Robin's ghost has been reported near a brook, known locally as Robin's Brook, and the blows of his ghostly axe have been heard at a distance.

Coggeshall Abbey
This pallid wrinkled monk walks silently around the Abbey with a lit taper, before leaving and making its way along the old lanes towards the Blackwater river.

47 Church Street
Once an inn, people in the building have reported doors that open and close without cause, odd smells, and a strange mist that crosses the base and top of the stairs

RETURN OF GEOFFREY DE MANDEVILLE

East Barnet and South Mimms in North London are two suburbs known for being leafy, calm and comfortable, and yet are classed as 'haunted lands' by many researchers. Within this reliatively small area there are hundreds of reports of ghosts and paranormal activity.

A thousand years ago these haunted lands were heavily wooded and were a part of a larger area including Chipping or High Barnet- where the Battle of Barnet took place. Most of this land was once owned by the Abbot of St Albans but in his resistance William the Conquerer, he lost the southern part of his lands to the Bishop of London.

One of the knights who fought alongside William the Conquerer at Hastings was Geoffrey de Mandeville from Dieppe in France. After the battle he was given large swaithes of land across Essex, Middlesex and adjoining counties. He became one of ten knights who were the highest ranking in England, however fortunes changed with his son William. In 1100 William was the Constable of the Tower of London and unfortunately one of his prisoners, Ranulf Flambard escaped. This had great repercussions for the de Mandevilles and William, as punishment, King Henry I confiscated William's three richest estates, Barnet included.

William's son Geoffrey set about to recover the family's fortunes through manipulation and political manoeuvring. By 1141 it began to pay off and Sir

Geoffrey was the premier baron of England. He was known for his ruthlessness and he created many powerful enemies, one of which became the King. Geoffrey played the political game wrongly just once, and paid for it dearly. During the battles between Stephen and Matilda, Geoffrey changed sides several times dependant on who was in the most powerful position at the time. This was a battle for the crown, so Geoffrey had to chose well, sadly like many barons of the time he picked Matilda. In 1143 after Stephen's release from prison and coronation, the earl was arrested by the King. Threatened with execution, Geoffrey surrendered his castles and estates to King Stephen and in reaction, he launched a rebellion.

For over a year Sir Geoffrey operated as a rebel mainly in the fen country, however he was besieged by King Stephen meeting a bloody death in September 1144. Because he was excommunicated, his body was denied burial by all churches, except one. His corpse was wrapped in lead and taken to the Templar Church in London where his effigy can still be seen today.

Why Geoffrey haunts East Barnet's Oak Hill Park and only appears at Christmas time no one knows for sure, however there have been dozens of witness to the ghost of a mediaeval knight appearing in full armour on horseback.

In 1926 the "clanking ghost" of Geoffrey hit the headlines after a night watchmen's experience were read out as a part of the East Barnet district councillors' minutes. The night watchmen in question had been working in Oak Hill Park during the recent road workings. However a week before Christmas he witnessed a figure enveloped in a long military cloak standing near a building that stands in the park. The night watchman observed the ghost long enough to realise that the cloak was actually see through and the figure within it was a skeleton. The councillors put forward the motion that the night watchmen should have some form of increased wage due to the issues he was experiencing! Another watchman asked to take over the former's shift began to shake like a leaf and refused to take over.

Interestingly the building where the night watchman had his experience was previously a part of the East Barnet workhouse that was founded in the early 1700s. "The Shanty" as the building was known has been known for many years to be haunted both by the "clanking ghost" and apparently mistreated children who were of punished by being shut up in the cellars below. The children's ghosts remain on sight after some of the children were lost in the vast underground passages, never to be seen again. At the time of the roadworks in 1926 many people expected the workmen involved to bring to light long-hidden secrets connected with the old workhouse.

After the newspaper reports of the night watchman's encounter with Sir Geoffrey, many journalists took to ghost hunting in the park. A Western Times journalist wrote; "Even the prospect of handsome photographs in the illustrated papers failed to tempt shy Geoffrey into the upper air today....In fact every effort to trace him since the debate with a view to ascertaining where he was a sufficiently disagreeable person to warrant extra payment to the night watchman had proved vain. Nevertheless local residents believe Geoffrey is lurking about somewhere in the neighbourhood."

Two years later great expectation had built for Geoffrey's return at Christmas, and on Christmas Eve he did appear.

"A few minutes before twelve o'clock near the old parish church at East Barnet, I saw in the distance a vague figure dressed in a heavy cloak, moving towards me from the direction of the Farm Home. I stood still and waited for this to approach, but suddenly it seemed to pass through a wall and disappear in the fields in the direction of Trent Barnet. As I waited and listened I distinctly heard sounds like the clanking of spurs but saw nothing more of the strange figure."

The witness, not named in the report was allegedly part of a ghost hunt organised by the New Barnet Research Society. The group sent members to be posted each night in different parts of the park to observe any ghostly activity.

When asked if the society would use force to rid the park of the ghost, they replied, "the purpose of the Research Society is to get into communication with the ghost quietly and try, if possible; to find out why Sir Geoffrey's spirit remains earthbound."

A year later the New Barnet Research Society are reported to undertake an even larger ghost hunt of Barnet and South Mimms, due to the reports of Rev. Allen Hay, a vicar who had an experience with a supernatural presence in his bedroom (?!) and a relative of his met a ghost of an Elizabethan woman in the village hall. Even South Mimms church at the time was alleged to be haunted by a clergyman dressed in white robes walking from the chancel and through a wall.

Due to the increase of sightings of Sir Geoffrey in the area at Christmas, the society decided to ban the press, other paranormal investigators and even asked police to regulate the queues of thousands of visitors armed with cameras and flash lamps wanting to see Sir Geoffrey.

Leading up to the ghost hunt there has been several reports of activity include the dogs in the neighbourhood becoming very restless at nightfall and a woman reporting over two successive nights the sound of muffled drums coming from the park.

With the ghost hunt cloaked in secrecy we don't know if Geoffrey once again made his return to the Park, however in 1932 the park had such a reputation that a local Justice of the Peach described Church Hill Road, which runs by the Park as "The Ghost's Promenade".

Another ghost hunt took place at Christmas a reporter wrote, "I, as with many others, gathered in the old village to await the arrival of the ghostly visitor. The night was cold and cloudy. There was a woodland copse in the background. As we stood, staring, there was a sudden break in the clouds and there could be seen clearly a figure in armour – Sir Geoffrey de Mandeville.

Jack Hallam in his book "Ghosts of London" claims that the first vigil after World War II brought nearly four hundred ghost hunters from all parts of London, sadly the only thing they saw that night was the mist swirl through the trees and along the gully known as Pym's Brook.

Although there are still reports of "clanking" and a cloaked figure in the park, as East Barnet press recently printed, "Headless hounds, decapitated bodies, spectres in the trees - the list of ghostly experiences at Oak Hill Park in East Barnet seems to go on and on."

YORK – BRITAIN'S MOST HAUNTED CITY

As one of the oldest cities in Britain, York stands head and shoulders above other cities that claim to be the most haunted. Every street, alley and even pub seems to have a chilling ghost story to tell, often plied by one of the many speakers from a "Ghost Walk".

Throughout Summer Ghost Walks take place guiding the curious through York's murderous and wretched past. Tales of lost love, the black plague, deadly duels and above all revengeful ghosts, excite and chill thousands of people every year.

So not to spoil your possible visit to York, I will introduce some of the less known ghost stories of York.

In the winter of 1879, a barrister working the Northern Circuit, arrived in York, as he tells us in the "Leisure Hour" magazine, "after a freezing ride from London, looking forward to a warm sitting and bedroom at the old York lodgings. At last we found the "Judge's House."

On entering the house, the barrister found that only the Judge and his Marshal were in residence and that the rest of the bedrooms were available.

After a large meal, the barrister retired to bed and fell fast asleep. At two o'clock in the morning, he woke suddenly with his heart thumping as he says "150 to the minute and with a vague and undefinable terror possessing him".

There was a terrible sensation of someone being in the room besides himself. He then heard footsteps walking across the room to the door. A loud cry shouted "Henry", then again and again it shouted "Henry". It seemed to be coming from the lower part of the house, as if someone was calling from the bottom of the stairs. The footsteps in his room walked towards the stairs and then he heard voices talking, a scuffle and then a silencing loud shriek.

Soon after he heard the heavy stumbling of wounded person walking back into the room, falling heavily on the floor. The Barrister then lost unconsciousness with fright.

The next morning, he awoke with to the sound of the servant trying to open his bedroom door, to bring him hot water but the door was locked.

At breakfast, the barrister spoke to the housekeeper who admitted after a little hesitation that the room he slept in was supposed to be haunted.

The room had not been slept in for over fifty years but because the other rooms were not ready for the guest and that she wanted to see if the ghost would return, she put him in that room.

The story of the room begins over a hundred and fifty years earlier, when a strange Judge was in charge of the York Assizes. With him as Marshal was his orphan nephew, a young man of great expectations who was heir to the Judge.

The Judge's butler slept in the next room to the Judge, one night he woke by the sound of the Judge walking to the young man's room.

Outside the door, the Judge began to call his nephew's name three times, "Henry, Henry, Henry!" A door opened and then the butler heard a struggle, and a cry of pain. Then steps were heard returning back down the staircase.

The next morning the young Marshal was found lying on the floor curled up in death with a deeply inflicted knife-wound in his chest.

The Judge took the enquiry in his own hands and gave the verdict as suicide.

Strange noises and shadows were often seen and heard in the room of Henry's death until it was locked and left for over a hundred and fifty years.

Now the Judge's house is no more, and with it the ghost and its tragic story.

York holds a strange tradition of headless ghosts. This may hark back to the days of Celtic worship of the Head. The Celts would keep the head of their chieftain or rivals, believing that their spirit is retained in the skull.

One headless ghost haunts the Churchyard of the Holy Trinity Church in Goodramgate. Although records show that no headless men were buried in that churchyard or church, the ghost still appears to this day.

One legend may explain the sightings. In 1569 the Earls of Northumberland and Westmoreland rebelled against the Queen Elizabeth I. The rebellion was suppressed and the Earl of Northumberland captured two years later.

A scaffold was built on the pavement at the end of the Shambles and on the 22nd of August 1572, the Earl was beheaded.

The body was buried in St Crux's church, while his head was set upon a pole on Micklegate Bar as a warning to other rebels. The head stayed there until 1574 when it was mysteriously stolen, disappearing from York and history.

York Folklore claims that one of the Earl's retainers took the head and buried it in the churchyard of Holy Trinity.

The ghost first appeared in St Crux's churchyard, which now is covered by pavement and shops. When this land was taken, the ghost moved to haunt the burial ground of St Saviour's. The ghost, obviously restless then began to appear in the churchyard of Holy Trinity.

The ghost could be that of an older memory, in 1469 Roger Layton was beheaded and buried in Holy Trinity Church, could it be his ghost wandering the churches of York?

One of the strangest ghost stories of York is that of the "Burning Babe".

Sometime ago, early last century, new drains were installed in the Precentor's Court, turning up hundreds of human bones. The ground previously being the part of York Cathedral's burial yard.

One night a young lady visited a house on Precentor's Court to talk to the occupants.

It was a dark winter's night and the lady knocked for a long time until the door finally opened.

There in the doorway stood a small figure of a small child surrounded by flames. The lady stood back in amazement, the figure grew and expanded until it filled the doorway. The lady ran away, collapsing at another house. There she was tendered for and recovered to tell her story.

The occupants of the house explained to her that house had been empty for over a month, the family was away on holiday. The records of York offer no explanation of the sighting or appearance.

One of York's hidden ghostly treasures is the Black Swan Public House on Peasholme Green. This is the oldest pub in York, dating from the 16th Century but its ghosts are from more recent times. Bar staff claim regularly to see a young lady in a white flowing dress. Her long, flaxen hair glows slightly as she walks past the stairs.

Another ghost is that of a Victorian gentleman who walks up the warped wooden staircase of the public house, often tutting or fidgeting, as if waiting for someone or something. One staff member, while locking up, followed the ghost up the stairs believing it was a drinker, only to discover he had vanished when he reached the top of the stairs.

The true secret of the Black Swan is in the walls of the main room, on the second level of the pub. The wooden panelling dating back to the 17th Century has thousands of grotesque figures and demons imprinted in to the varnishing. This room has been the secret meeting place for esoteric societies through the years. Nobody knows who painted them or their purpose, but take your time and see the observing figures of the Black Swan.

THE GHOSTS OF STREET HOUSE

A Personal Record by Francis Mariott-Wood..

About 1854 my father bought what was then called "Street House," an old Abbey Grange about a mile and a half from Glastonbury. The house had belonged to a Captain Festing, and owing to its reputation for being haunted, had been empty many years. My father had, however, made up his mind there was no truth in the tales told, but that it was to the interest of a farmer close at hand to keep it empty, as he had some way of making money out of the splendid walled-fruit gardens, which covered about an acre, and of otherwise entertaining himself and his friends. The farmer's sons were most disreputable young fellows, and several times tried to terrify the maids. Indeed, we had been told we should not be able to keep any. Certainly the house was most desolate, excepting on the south side, where it was clad in wisteria, magnolia, and jessamine, and in front of this my father laid out an Italian garden.

The mansion was in three parts, each shut off from the other by large doors. The front was Georgian, and the middle Tudor. The original Grange was in the rear, and consisted of a large stone-flagged kitchen, a servant's hall, and other rooms. Beyond these were a fine dairy and a scullery, which led out into a large yard, with walls quite twelve feet high, with sloping ledges a-top, forming a place where monks could walk up and down in seclusion. No one spoke to us of ghosts, the servants having been warned it would mean instant dismissal if they did so. Our cook, however, many years after told us she used often to see a little old man in a leathern jerkin, with knee breeches, in the old scullery. I may add that in spite of some strange happenings we lived at Street House for a quarter of a century in great happiness.

There is a tale that when the poor Abbot was hanged on Tor Hill, the monks and nuns fled by the secret way to Street House, destroying the passage as they went along, but their enemies found out what had happened, and walled up the outlet, leaving the unhappy victims to perish.

There was alleged to be another subterranean passage from Street House to Sharpham Park, in Walton, where the Abbot was taken, but we never discovered its entrance, unless it were somehow through a well under the stone at the back door. This habit of putting a well in front of the front door seems to hold still in Somersetshire. It is possible they are not really wells, but rather contrivances to cloak the entrances to the subterranean passages with which the country seemed riddled at one time. Why they should have been made is, of course, a question. As the country round Glastonbury up to the middle ages was much of a morass, possibly such passages made it easier for the monks and nuns to get from one to another of the rest houses, dry, and, so far as those who were "enclosed " were concerned, without breaking cloister bounds.

Until early in the last century there was a stone in the wall of St. Benedict's Church, Glastonbury, bearing the names of those owners of land who had to lend men and work to repair a certain portion of the sea wall. Such stones may be seen at the present day on the Green Beach at Clevedon, measuring out what it was the duty of each landowner to maintain. Some of the farmers near Glastonbury objected very much to this task, and one night someone got into the church and stole the stone. This did not, however, stop the tax, which was then, and is now, put on to the rates.

The tale that there was treasure hidden at Street House also always was believed. A certain Mr. Hawkins who wanted to buy the house, owned openly that it was for the purpose of pulling it down so as to find the treasure. As, however, he only offered four hundred pounds for a place worth five thousand he cannot have had much faith in its worth!

Our first warning that all was not quite as it should be with the house did not happen till some time after we arrived, when some cousins came from the North of England to visit us - a brother, two sisters, and their maid. They were wealthy people, and accustomed to luxury, and the sisters were not in the habit of sharing a bed. It was set down to their not being comfortable, therefore, and wishing to make excuses, when on the morning after their arrival, they announced that they must leave that day. The sisters said they had been frightened out of their wits by a nun, who sat in their room, and was quite visible. They had called their maid in from next door, and though they had tried the effect of moving various pieces of furniture they had not been able to get rid of her. Nothing would persuade them to stay longer with us, and much to my father's indignation they left. Their brother had been as much alarmed by noises at the head of his bed as they had been, but these could be accounted for, as there was a blocked-up window there, for my father was putting heavy plate glass windows in the library underneath, and no doubt plaster had got loose and was falling down. They all departed, however, convinced that the house was haunted, and forty years later the sisters declared that they always shuddered when they thought of that room.

On examination it proved that there was a wall seven feet thick there. My father was employing a Bath firm to paper the front hall, and told them to open the wall, so as to see if there was anything in it. They only took out one stone, and then refused to do more, saying there was a curse on anyone who meddled with it. Possibly this was a result of the superstition made use of in "The Ingoldsby Legends," but my father must have had some sympathy with the idea, for though a very determined man as a rule, he did not insist upon further investigation, and the mystery of that wall was never cleared up in our time, nor, so far as I know, afterwards.

It was several years before we heard anything more of the supernatural, and though the green room was often slept in, no-one saw or heard anything. I was seventeen before the next happening took place, and had "come out" at a grand ball we had given, but was still kept chiefly in the schoolroom to continue my education. It was the last day of the holidays, and I was making breakfast in our most desolate schoolroom, when my youngest brother came in, and said very nervously:

"I have something I want to tell you, but. . . . you must promise not to tell Charles."

I promised, and he said: "Such an odd thing happened last night. I woke up, and saw a big white dog sitting opposite the stove."

"Well, what did you do?"

"I sat up and looked at him, and as he seemed doing no harm, I lay down and went to sleep again."

"Only a dream," I said. "You had better not tell Charles, for he would only laugh at you."

He went away, muttering, "It was a real dog all the same."

He had scarcely gone when Charles came in, and looked round.

"Where's Dick?" he asked.

"Just gone down the stone path."

"Well, I want to tell you something, but you must not tell Dick."

"Not till you let me," I said, feeling rather excited.

"Such an odd thing happened last night. I woke up and saw a large white dog sitting opposite the stove. Whilst I was looking at it, it got up and went out of the room, by the door. I suddenly remembered I had left the door locked on getting into bed. I jumped up; it was still locked. I opened it and looked down the passage, but there was nothing there. But I saw the thing as clearly as I clearly as I see you now, for the moon was shining brightly..."

"You must tell Dick," I exclaimed, as I ran to the window to call him back.

On comparing notes, the brothers, who slept at different ends of a long narrow room in the oldest part of the house, found they had seen the same weird animal like a bulldog from their accounts.

We went down to prayers in a great state of excitement, and the story was received with considerable wrath by my father, who stopped the servants as they trooped in to prayers, and said, sternly:

"I find someone has been talking about ghosts to my children. We are not going to be turned out of the house by foolish tales. The next time I hear anything of this sort you will all pack up and go. I never threaten twice."

We all assured him we had heard nothing about ghosts from them, and received such scoldings that we really began to think there was nothing in it. On the return of our governess that night we told her, laughing, what had happened.

"It's all very well to laugh," she said, " but you mark my words, there will be a death in the family within three weeks."

"But Miss S - we exclaimed, " You always say you do not believe in ghosts."

"Neither do I, hut I do believe in these omens," and she proceeded to tell us of various houses dowered with such uncanny spectres.

Of course, it was very wrong of her, but her words were startlingly verified. I was taking a drawing lesson about three weeks later, and we heard a noise. Miss S said: "That must be 'Ruski' chasing a rat; would you like to go and see?"

I ran off, and looked over the banisters of the old stairs, and what I saw smote me with horror and dismay. For there were some of the men carrying my father's dead body into his study! He had been to Bath for the waters, as he was suffering from dropsy, but had returned so much better that our doctor, who had seen him that very day, said, "Sir, I never saw such an improvement. I have not seen you looking so well since you have been in England."

Well, after my father's death my mother moved from the modern part of the house into what was called "The Green Room," the apartment where our Kershaw cousins saw the ghost. It faced north, and was dismally furnished. The paper was a dull drab, with the pattern so worn that there was only a shadow of it. The curtains were of a sage green colour, with great sprawling patterns of what stood for leaves; the carpet also was of a dingy hue.

The Russian war in the Crimea had terrified my father - lest he might a second time lose his fortune and the results of ten years of hard work - and he had stopped all building and repairs, inside and out, and the house was never fully furnished. This may have had something to do with the dreary look of the room, although my mother changed the hangings more than once. But none of those changes hindered us from often seeing a shadowy appearance of a monk. One of us always slept in my mother's room; generally it was my lot, and again and again I have wakened to see a grey robed form by my side, with hand stretched out as if in benediction.

Sometimes my mother would call out, "Oh, the man the man," at which he always disappeared. Personally, I was not at all afraid of him, and prided myself on going about the house in the dark, but on one occasion it cost me dear. I was passing through the oaken doors which shut the old part of the house from the new, when my youngest sister, who was coming up the stairs, with fatal presence of mind threw her candlestick at me, utterly ruining a quite new silk dress I had on. She said she thought it was a burglar, but I spell that word GHOST!

My mother once saw the shadowy figure of a nun thrown on the wall. She described it as wearing -what in Cheshire, her native county, is called "a mutch" upon her head. A maid was sleeping in her room at the time, and together they got up and moved everything that could cast a shadow about, but it made no difference. After a while the shade disappeared, and she never saw it again.

One night four years after my father's death we were roused by a violent knocking at the back door, and huddling on some clothes went down and called through the door to ask what was the mutter.

" 'Tis James, Miss," came in a rather quavery voice. "My wife a zin thicky white dog, an be like to die o' fright. Do ye come to the lodge and see ef so be ye can comfort she."

The lodge for the coachman was only a stone's throw from the back door, so, accompanied by our cook, I went along.

Polly was as white as a sheet, and trembling like a leaf, and called out as soon as she saw me:

"O lor Miss, I've a seen the white dog; be I agooin' to die?"

"It's very conceited of you to think he comes for any but the family," I said. "You know the other time when Emily and Foot saw him it was for Mr. Wood. No harm happened to either of them."

It was a chance thought, but a happy one. The colour returned, and Polly was no worse for her fright, nor did anything happen; but I really believe she might have died of fright but for my happy inspiration.

One other uncanny thing we had at Street. This was a phantom carriage which from time to time used to come up the drive, and stop in front of the front door. Many times we have run out to see who had arrived at such an untimely hour, for this visitation generally took place about nine o'clock at night, but there was never anything to be seen. We tried to reason ourselves into thinking that it was a passing vehicle in the road, but there was scarcely any vehicular traffic, and the factory and Parsonage were between us and the road, so what caused this delusion I cannot guess.

Street House's History

After reading this tale I decided to check out Street House's history to see if there would be any links with the Benedictine monk or white dog as vividly described by Frances. There is no doubt that the land has its links with the monks, between 1066 and 1547 the land was owned by Glastonbury Abbey which was under Benedictine orders. Could the ghost at Frances' bed be one of the monks from this era?

Later the estate passed into the hands of Edward, Duke of Somerset in 1547, over the next forty years the manor and estates passed into various owners and sub-letters until in 1591 when the manor was sold to trustees of Sir Christopher Hatton. Sir Hatton who died the same year leaving as his heir his nephew Sir

William Hatton of Newport. Over the next two hundred years the house and estates pass through several families including Dyer, Strode and Howe.

In 1823 Mary Howe divided her estate between her cousins, Charles Brown who was left Street House and the farm. Within six years Charles Brown died and the property passed to his brother Joseph. A pattern emerges after the property is sold to George Tucson, and six years later it sold to Frances' father Charles Wood. Sadly, four years later Charles dies (as described in the story) and the ownership passes to his wife Lydia for life. In 1878 Charles Provost bought it from the Reverend. R. N. Wood. In 1890 Provost, who had renamed the house Abbey Grange, sold the house to James Clark and, known as the Grange, it remained part of the Clark estate in 1999.

The only question left why was Street House visited by a presage of death that manifested itself as a white dog?

THE OLD NURSING HOME

I thought I would share just a few things with you that I have experienced over the past fourteen years working as a carer in the same nursing home in Wiltshire. The home is a very old but beautiful mansion set in large grounds and in the past not only used as a private family home but also, during the war, was used as a rehabilitation centre for the soldiers who were injured.

I have experienced many things while on duty both during the day and at night. The most common sighting from patients, passed and present is of a Lady in a Blue Dress. Many patients have mentioned her not only to me but also colleagues.

It always seems to be patients who reside in a certain corridor of the home that mention her i.e. they would ring their bell and ask whether I could make the Lady in the Blue Dress a cup of tea. What I found strange was that she was always described to us as 'the lady in the blue dress'.

Obviously I thought that this lady had to have been a passed patient of ours who resided in this part of the house and was wearing her favourite blue dress. This was until the summer almost three years ago now, I was walking along the 'haunted' corridor when I saw the sister on duty pass around the corner up some stairs. When I called out to the sister for some advice she replied from a different location. I immediately turned the corner where the person I saw vanished into thin air! I then realised that the lady in the blue dress was not an old patient of ours whatsoever but a senior nurse!

I saw her again in the same location about three months later this time she passed a doorway about two foot away from me, I knew immediately that it was her as I recognised the footwear. I can't remember hearing her or what made me look over my shoulder at the time, but there she was. On both sightings I only saw her from the waist down, not because she was headless or anything of the sort but just because of the angle I caught sight of her.

She wasn't at all what I had expected i.e. see through and ghostly but quite the opposite, she was three dimensional like you and I, she wore black tights and black lace up shoes and she walked briskly and both times vanished.

We also have mischievous ghosts which do scare me a little bit to say the least, and they get up to almost anything, again it is in certain rooms and is often dismissed by the nurses as a confused patient. It seems that some ghosts crave for attention more than others and are very persistent and let us know that it isn't the patient that is confused!

Early one evening myself and three other nurses sat taking a report from the sister when a resident rang for assistance. I answered the call, three levels up to the top of the building, I used the lift as the stairs are sometimes quite creepy. The male resident complained that his TV would not stay on one channel and kept switching through all four. I reminded him how to use his remote control and how if he pressed any of the buttons that the TV would change channels.

Happy with that I returned to the rest of the staff, two minutes later he rang again. I went again to him and he had the same complaint so I put the TV on the channel he wanted to watch and placed the remote way out of his reach on the dresser to prevent any further confusion.

He rang again and when I arrived the same old story about the TV and as I was about to leave, before my very own eyes the TV was flicking quickly through all four channels, I removed the plug told him it was faulty and legged it to the rest of the staff!

No sooner had I got down stairs to explain to the other staff the lady in the room next to him rang her bell.

This time feeling nervous I took the other three nurses with me to investigate. As we passed the man's room his door slammed shut in front of us all and as if that wasn't enough the lady in the next room who was ringing was fast asleep in her chair and her bell was about four foot away from her, on her bed!

Footsteps have also been heard late at night when everything is quiet, it is as if someone is doing a check of certain rooms. You can hear them walk then stop, then walk and stop until they reach the end of the corridor then they walk the whole length back and you can hear this most nights about two or three times.

I have saved the scariest story until last. As a night worker I am quite familiar with the goings on and confident to walk around in the dark (some nights I get a bit spooked mind you) and have been known to play a few tricks on some colleagues who are not so keen of the dark.

Now there is one place I will not go in the nursing home and that is the attic which we use as a storeroom and I believe is haunted more than any other place in the home.

One night I had to retrieve something from the attic and took a colleague (who I have previously played silly little tricks on) with me, she was nervous so I had to act the 'big brave I am'. As I entered the attic the door slammed behind me leaving me in side and her outside. She thought I had done it and I thought she had done it to teach me a lesson.

The door was locked and she was trying to tell me she couldn't unlock it, of course still thinking this was a get your own back, I thought she was pulling my leg!

I have to admit I was terrified when she began to panic and realised it wasn't her doing at all. I was stood in the corner too scared to look behind in case something was going to come and get me!

She passed the key under the door for me to try and unlock it but it just wouldn't budge. It would move freely in the lock but just wouldn't unlock! With sheer fear my colleague kicked the door open and when we tried to unlock it after, it worked just fine! This taught me a lesson and I was never a naughty girl again.

A to Z of BRITAIN'S SCARIEST GHOSTS

The question of the existence of ghosts continues to be a controversial one, yet it is not very long ago that the British Tourist Authority claimed that there were some 10,000 hauntings in the UK. Ghosts have been accepted since Stone Age man started drawing spirits and gods on his cave walls, and the Romans were writing about them long before they conquered Britain. It is, however, this country that has more genuine or at least more reports of hauntings than any other.

Alton, Hampshire
St Lawrence's church was the scene of a bloody battle during the Civil War when Royalists were besieged here, their colonel making a heroic last stand in the pulpit and putting six or seven Roundheads to the sword before falling himself, with sixty of his own troops around him. This savagery is sometimes re-enacted in the church, though the conflict is heard rather than seen.

Nearby Crown Hotel is haunted by a mistreated dog that was killed when it was smashed against a hearth. In the 1960's workmen found the bones of a dog behind a false wall by the chimney breast. The whimpers and scratching of the dog are still heard.

Bedlay Castle, Strathclyde
Bedlay is a beautiful and atmospheric typically Scottish castle that was built in the 1100's. Once it was the palace of the Bishops of Glasgow, one of whom, Bishop Cameron died after drowning in a fishpond in

the grounds. For the last seven hundred years his ghost has been seen wandering the building, slowly fading through time.

Bettiscombe Manor, near Lyme Regis in Dorset
The Manor houses the skull of a West Indian Slave brought back during the 17th Century. The spirit of the dead man would not rest in the nearby churchyard so the skull has been kept at the house to avoid the terrible hauntings following his burial.

Blackfriars Priory, Gloucester
There are many ruined buildings which because of their state are automatically thought to be haunted, but one that seems to have a genuine ghost is Blackfriars Priory, in Gloucester. Whilst working on the huge task of restoring the priory, workmen from the Department of the Environment have seen the figure of a monk gliding across the cloister area.

A previously unknown 'dungeon' was opened in 1969 and found to contain the skeleton of a young child, but whether there is some connection with this and the appearance of the phantom is unknown.

Brighton Road, Handcross in Brighton
A strange road ghost has become more and more apparent with its activity on this stretch of road. In 2005, a local businesswoman was shocked when it jumped in front of her car. She said: "It was so strange - There were no other cars around so it couldn't have been car headlights, yet I saw three bright lights and this hazy figure."

Bradford Ghost Terror
A ghostly terror struck the suburbs of Bradford in September 1926. Over a period of several nights a ghost appeared to the residents of the Brierley Housing Estate, often frightening and even attacking lonely women.

The Bradford Ghost made his first appearance early September, the first witnesses saw the ghost walking around the streets of Bradford and described it as being a white male figure at least six feet two inches in height. The ghost, it was claimed also had a "wonderful agility" and ran as fast as an Olympic champion!

Buckingham Old Gaol
Situated in the heart of the town of Buckingham stands the majestic Old Gaol. It has served the county for nearly two hundred years and has seen some strange characters come and go. The last few years have seen an amazing increase in activity at the Old Gaol with many of the visitors reporting the presence of something nasty in one of the cells. The cells have an uncanny knack of changing in atmosphere with minutes of entering and often becoming unbearable.

Many visitors have witnessed a small child walking along the top corridor of the Old Gaol near to the Jailer's office. Other incidents have included a cell doors that slams closed and during a recent investigation a white figure was witnessed.

Burton Agnes Hall, Yorkshire
After being attacked and beaten by robbers, Anne Griffiths in her dying breaths expressed the wish that her head should be buried in the home that she so much loved. Nevertheless her family buried her in the village churchyard.

After the funeral, terrifying groans and poltergeist activity such as doors slamming and crashes were heard around the house. The dead girl's body was exhumed and her skull was exhumed and bricked up in a wall off the staircase. Although in recent times the skull has been on display without any side effects.

Callow, Hereford
Callow Farm next to the Church was once an inn where travellers were often robbed and murdered, their bodies being taken across two fields to be hidden in a cottage that was pulled down many years ago. On Halloween night, the building reappears in a ghostly, ethereal form and figures carrying corpses have also been seen stumbling across the fields.

The Chequers Pub, Amersham
The pub is haunted by no less than nine ghosts. These are thought to be the spirits of men and women held at the Chequers overnight before being sent to the gallows. In the room where they were held, sightings of a woman dressed in white and a chimney sweep are so common that it is the only bedroom in the pub not rented out to guests.

Chagford, Devon
The Three Crowns Hotel has a ghostly visitor in the shape of a Cavalier. He wanders the corridors and rooms at night, and they even know he is called Sidney – from a painting hanging in the bar. On the outskirts of Chagford is Blackaton Brook, the phantom sound of sword fighting and pistol firing between Cavaliers and Roundheads has been heard many times here.

Clifton Hampden, Oxfordshire
The ghost of Sarah Fletcher haunts a house called "The Courtiers", so attractive is the ghost that many have fallen in love with her. If you decide to ignore her, she will only become a nuisance and upset your stay. Her husband, a naval Captain left her and tried to marry a wealthy heiress. At his wedding, Sarah announced he was committing bigamy and stopped the marriage. The Captain went back to sea and was never seen again, while Sarah, heart-broken, hung herself from the curtain rail of her four-poster bed.

Cowdray House, Midhurst, Sussex
This ruinous house is one of Southern England's most important early Tudor palaces, built from 1520 and partly destroyed by fire in 1793. With a history of being cursed, tragic loss of life to male heirs and lots of ghosts, the house is one of the most scenic and spookiest places to visit in the UK. The crypt is haunted by someone who lost their life in the great fire who is always pleased to interact with visitors – is it really the ghost that touches people and blows in their faces? Inside the ruins is the white lady who wanders the ruins looking for her lost love.

Crown Hotel, Wells

There has been a catalogue of incidents at this city centre hotel - some stranger than others. Figures have been seen walking along corridors, heard banging around in rooms and caught disrupting the dining room. Several members of staff saw a dark figure in the hotel's front bar on camera after hours but there was no one there. Another staff member watched as something pushed candles and knocked napkins off tables.

But perhaps the most bizarre thing that has happened has been the appearance of black barley seeds in large quantities in some of the bedrooms. No one knows how they got there or where they came from!

Devil's Nags, Pembrokeshire

The "Nags" are actually two ancient standing stones in a field called "Cot Moor" believed to be haunted by a hell hound. Sometime in the past a walker witnessed a dog "more terrible than he had ever seen", so he picked up a stone to scare the animal away but a circle of fire surrounded the dog and it disappeared!

Dudley Castle, Dudley

For over nine hundred years a fortification has stood on the hill that over looks the Black Country. For the last four years I have been able to chart the experiences of Fright Nights attendees and local witness recollections.

The castle has two reoccurring ghosts, the Black Monk and the Grey Lady. The Monk has been seen in all areas of the castle and is claimed to be an evil force, with many people being upset by his sudden appearances.

The Grey Lady only appears at the castle keep and has been witnessed more than any other ghost in the West Midlands! During the last sighting she walked past the witness, stood gazing around and promptly disappeared. I have been lucky enough to collect over twenty five individual ghost sightings at Dudley Castle and the list still increases.

Dunham Massey Hall, Greater Manchester
Now a National Trust location and open to the public, the Hall once had a reputation of being a notoriously haunted location. The eighteenth century hall replaced an Elizabethan manor house. When the present house was being built its architect mysteriously fell to his death. Many suspected that he was pushed from the roof after a dispute with the builders. His spectre still wanders the grounds and house.

East Bergholt Friary, Suffolk
Originally a Benedictine convent called St Mary's Abbey, the Friary is said to be haunted and indeed there is an atmosphere there which extends across the road to East Bergholt Church. During the Second World War soldiers were stationed at the Friary and at that time one particular door which led into the sergeant's mess would unlatch itself every night at ten minutes to eleven and open to a distance of about 8 inches; a distinct drop in air temperature would precede this apparent phenomenon and soldiers playing cards

in the room would purposely stop at this time to wait for the door to open; each night it would regularly 'oblige'.

Fountains Abbey, Yorkshire
A ghostly choir has been heard chanting in the abbey's Chapel of Nine Altars but the most interesting ghost resides in nearby Fountains Hall. Built by Sir Stephen Proctor, a blue ghost, that of his daughter who witnessed her father's evil doings and remains at the hall for eternity. An Elizabethan man has been seen emerging from the panelling in the stone hall.

Galleries of Justice, Nottingham
Originally called "The Shire Hall", the building has served Nottingham for over five hundred years as an administration centre and jail. It is an amazing building with a labyrinth of corridors, cells and caves. Sightings include a sitting gentleman in the reception, a young man appearing in the criminal court (its alleged he was hung in there), a smelly ghost in the Night Cell who likes to grab women's ankles and a poltergeist in the Chapel. Many things have been witnessed at the Galleries of Justice and its atmosphere is very unique.

Gilmerton Cove, Edinburgh
The Cove is series of hand carved passageways and chambers that lie below ground to the south of Gilmerton crossroads. The origins of Gilmerton Cove, which after extensive archaeological and historical research, still remain a mystery. With Gilmerton Cove being linked to a local "Hellfire Club" and the Knights Templars, there was no doubt that rumours of ghosts would persist. Over the years people have claimed to

hear phantom laughter and footsteps coming from the Cove, and yet it lies empty. The most terrifying ghost is that of a witch who is said to pull hair and push visitors who have religious views!

Highwaymen Ghosts
A remnant of times past, these ghostly riders of our roads still continue to appear and frighten motorists. The Todwick Highwayman is a figure of a man sitting on a dark horse, wearing a long flowing cape which spread out over the horse's rump.

Hook Green near Lamberhurst, Kent.
Stay away from this heavily haunted area of Kent! Nearby ruinous Bayham Abbey is haunted by phantom bells, ghostly voices and obviously monks. Visitors have often reported the smell of burning incense (not used here in over five hundred years) and of white monks walking the ruins. The road from Hook Green to Bell's Yew Green is haunted by a phantom car that disappears as you drive closer to it.

Horsell Common, Woking, Surrey
Horsell Woods and Common are haunted by various apparitions including a backpacker and a tall figure that walks from a nearby World War I graveyard. This year alone there have been six sightings of the mysterious backpacker who likes to walk in front of passers by.

Ickworth Rectory, Norfolk
Tales of missing church treasure and a ghostly black dog are often read about this strange little building. The ghost is that of Rev. Cyril Mitford who died of a

broken heart after his wife mysteriously disappeared a few weeks earlier. Within a few months of his death, Cyril was witnessed by the new rector walking in the room that he had died. For many years Cyril's ghost continued to visit the rectory and was seen by the whole family, however on one occasion his appearance drove the family's dog to madness.

Ilam Hall, Derbyshire
There have been two halls standing on this site, the first was built by the Port family in the 16th century but this was demolished by J.W. Russell to make way for his much grander hall of the 1820s. Most of the hall was demolished in the 1920s before Sir Robert McDougall bought the estate and donated it to the National Trust in 1934.

The Hall itself is now used by the Youth Hostel Association, but if you plan on staying be aware there are numerous ghosts haunting the location. The most active ghost is a white lady who has the habit of waking up people who are staying in the Youth Hostel. She has also been seen wandering the corridors and between the Church and the Italian Garden.

A phantom coach and horses is also said to be seen turning around in one of the old courtyards. Phantom coaches are usually completely black and may be a carriage or an actual hearse. The staff at the Hall have reported unusual occurrences including the curtains opening and closing by themselves and the spectre of a ghostly butler walking the corridors.

Kent Life Museum, Maidstone, Kent
This open air museum has several ghosts ranging from a farmhouse haunted by a woman who died holding her newborn baby in her arms, to an Oast House frequented by a young maiden who drowned in a nearby pond. The scariest ghost is that of a German pilot who was killed when his plane crashed into the museum's tearoom. To this day his bloodied ghost appears standing in the corner looking mournful.

Leosowe Castle
The castle was constructed in 1592 for an heir to the English throne – Ferdinando Stanley, who according to the Will of King Henry VIII was third in line to the throne if Queen Elizabeth I died without heir. Sadly Ferdinando was poisoned and never reached the crown and the castle was left to be passed from owner to owner, and now is a luxury hotel.

There are many recorded ghosts at Leasowe Castle but the most famous relates to a father and child being locked in a room to starve to death. The father, to save himself and his child from such a painful death killed his son and then committed suicide. For the last hundred years there have been reports of sightings of the ghostly pair walking near the "haunted room". Many of the staff of the hotel have received terrifying reports of activity from guests that have literally sent them running for the exit!

Lichfield Guildhall, Staffordshire
The Guildhall in Bore Street has been central to the government of the City for over 600 years, and in

former times was not only the meeting place of the Corporation but also at various times the court, prison, police station, theatre and fire station. The old prison for felons and debtors is at the rear of the building and has been in existence since 1553. From the prison various convicts have been condemned to be publicly hanged at the gallows.

Sightings of a dark figure looming at the rear of the Guildhall have often spooked cleaners and workers and does his reappearance coincide with the recent redevelopments. Another ghost witnessed is that of a lady who wanders in one of the main meeting rooms. It is alleged that she is the wife of a former Sheriff of Lichfield who was savagely murdered in the stairway leading to the jails underneath. Why she should appear in the meeting rooms is not known but her encounters often precede poltergeist activity.

Little Compton, Warwickshire
In the 1870's Mr Drane, the curate at St Denis's church became enamoured with a woman who sang in the choir. However the woman - Miss Fielding - favoured Captain Brandon who lived at the Grange. When they became engaged Miss Fielding asked Drane to perform the ceremony. He did so but after the ceremony he hanged himself in the belfry. Drane's ghost still walks the church and rings the bell on the anniversary of his death.

Mary King's Close, Edinburgh
Abandoned following the plague in 1645, Mary King's Close has been a location associated with the

paranormal for hundreds of years. In 1685, "Satan's Invisible World Discovered", a book that recorded a demonic parade of apparitions which forced locals to flee the Close in terror some years before.

Newton-le-Willows
Ghostly marching footsteps are said to be heard at Newton-le-Willows near Warrington during the month of August. It is thought that these sounds are the last few steps of Highlanders, fighting for the Royalist cause, who were caught and hanged on the spot by Cromwell's troops, in August, 1648.

Prestbury, Gloucestershire
A fantastic location for the ghost hunter, it has a Black Abbot that walks from the church at Easter, Christmas and on All Saints Day; a cavalier on horseback (the ghost of a messenger who was unseated by a rope across the road), and a knight in shining armour. A phantom shepherd haunts Swindon Lane, an elderly lady peers through the windows on Main Street and Mrs Preece's ghost in Mill Lane also causes a few scares.

The most scariest area is Cleeve Corner, a rambling old house by the church, and haunted by the ghost of a young bride who was strangled in her bed and those who sleep in the room run the danger of feeling themselves being throttled.

Reculver Towers, Kent
The twin towers of the former Roman fort of Reculver are a well-known landmark on the North Kent coast, it

is also a location that harbours some unusual hauntings including dark shadows and the sounds of a baby crying. The location that has a very strange and unusual presence about it that even in the middle of summer there is something unmistakeably "wrong".

Sandford Manor, Oxfordshire
Thomas de Saunford gave Sandford Manor to the Knights Templar in 1240. Nearby is Sandford Pool, a mysterious place where five undergraduates have been drowned – all from Christ Church College. There are more ghostly connections here – George Napier, a Jesuit in the time of Elizabeth I, was executed at Oxford and his head displayed on the college. It is rumoured that his ghost drives a coach from Temple Farm to Oxford every Christmas Eve seeking his lost head.

Scarborough Castle, Yorkshire
King Edward II's favourite, Piers Gaveston haunts Scarborough Castle after he was captured here and taken to Kenilworth Castle for execution. His headless ghost is malevolent and rushes at trespassers who unwisely visit the castle at night. The resort also has a Pink Lady, Lydia Bell, who haunts the street where she was murdered in 1804, and a black horse has haunted here since Norman times, appearing out of a thundercloud.

Scone Palace, Tayside
A very unusual ghost haunts the palace. On the south passage is the haunting of "Boring Walker", he is said to walk around the palace and is the cause of some of

the recent activity. Strangely at Scone the footsteps echo from a stone floor, whereas the south passage has a creaky wooden floor!

Sedgemoor, Somerset
In the district of Sedgemoor, Bawdrip is a haunted village with a very long pedigree. It's most famous ghost is that of Eleanor Lovell who died at the time of her marriage! Bawdrip Rectory seems to be the focus for the hauntings with witnesses claiming to have seen a lady in grey walking across the lawn. Paranormal activity always increased after Christmas, and one Vicar's family were driven to despair after living with heavy furniture being flung around by invisible forces. In more recent times Eleanor or the poltergeist seem more content to play with light switches and doors.

Shady Lane, Ashford in the Water, Derbyshire
Shady Lane heads to the next village of Longstone and has always been associated with hauntings. When I was younger we would regularly sit vigil on the lane looking for an obscure ghost. The Lane has a procession of twelve headless men carrying a coffin that is said to be empty. Why is it empty - because the space is there for you! If you see the ghost it is said that you will die within
the year.

Skegby Hall, Sutton in Ashfield
Now serving as the officers for the local council, Skegby Hall was once a school and originally a 14th century mansion. For countless years successive headmasters of the school witnessed the ghost as well

as a fair few pupils. The ghost is that of a funeral cortège with cowled monks carrying a coffin while singing a dirge. This scene was re-enacted over many years but recently there have been no reports since the school closed.

Smithills Hall near Bolton
Smithills Hall has its very own resident ghostly grey lady who has made several appearances in the past four years. A photograph taken some years ago by Insurance Agent Mr Allan Ridyard showed much more than he bargained for. The snap of his children is a nice one - except for the mysterious figure in grey alongside them.

St John's College, Oxford
In 1645, Archbishop Laud was beheaded for his belief in the church against Parliament and was buried beneath the altar in the chapel of his college. His ghost is unconventional. In its most spectacular form, it bowls its head towards the feet of anyone unlucky enough to meet it. In a quieter mode, he walks in the normal way but a few inches off the ground, probably reflecting the way the earth has settled over the centuries.

Washington Old Hall, Washington
Now owned by the National Trust, was built in the early 17th century on the site of an older building in which the Washington Family, ancestors of George Washington, had lived between 1183 and 1613. The phantom of a "Lady in a long grey dress" has been seen gliding along an upstairs corridor. She has been

described as resembling one of the portraits which hang in the Hall.

Woodchester Mansion, Gloucestershire

This deserted Mansion sits in a dark wooded valley and is seriously haunted. For over 200 years there have been reports of headless horsemen, flying coffins and a strange dwarf - and that's just outside!

The Mansion sits on a site that has house three other buildings and that just makes for a more intense experience. As with most mansions, it has the ghost of a white lady she is often seen on the first floor wandering backwards and forwards with the faint scent of perfume. Another ghost is that of a lady who attacks young women and a few hours after her appearance another ghost appears, that of a young man looking out of a window.

In the Chapel poltergeist activity has been witnessed, a large black dog and even a floating Victorian gentleman. So beware - the Mansion is bizarre, gothic and very strange!

Wilderhope Manor, Herefordshire

Dating from 1585, Wilderhope Manor is an unspoilt Elizabethan gabled manor house with many of its original features still intact. The house is virtually unaltered except for fine plasterwork ceilings, which were installed in the 17th century. The building is unfurnished except for a unique bow rack with room for 13 weapons over the hall fireplace.

There are many ghosts at Wilderhope Manor and the surrounding countryside, nearby on Wenlock Edge is a spot known as the 'Major's Leap'. This commemorates Thomas Smallman, the owner of Wilderhope Manor during the Civil War. He was a major in the Royalist Army and was caught by Cromwell's troops while carrying dispatches from Bridgnorth to Shrewsbury. He was imprisoned at Wilderhope Manor but escaped and fled on his horse. The fierceness of his captors' pursuit forced Smallman off the road and over Wenlock Edge. Although his horse was killed, a crab-apple tree broke the major's fall. His pursuers assumed that he was dead, but once they had left Smallman climbed up the hill and continued to Shrewsbury.

A writer spent a week's holiday at Wilderhope because he'd heard about the ghost of a cavalier who haunts the main hall. For the first night nothing happened but the following day when he was up on scaffolding painting the fine plaster ceiling he suddenly became aware of a tall figure standing in the doorway. At first he thought it was the warden checking up on him but then he noticed that the man was dressed in a full cloak, a floppy hat with a large plume, and thigh length boots. He then thought he was a visitor in fancy dress, but when he said 'Hello' all the visitor did was to raise his head slightly, before walking across the room and passing through a solid wall. He believed that he'd seen the ghost of Thomas Smallman.

The cavalier isn't the only ghost at the hall, indeed the most active is that of an innocent young girl who when approached smiles sweetly before screaming – a scream from hell.

Worthing, Sussex
Now a suburb of Worthing, Broadwater was once the home of an old oak tree called "The Midsummer Tree", On Midsummer's Eve, six skeletons were said to rise out of the ground and dance around the tree. In the 1860s, a young man witnessed the skeletons and was left in a state of shock.

Vampires
Believe it or not, Britain has a number of locations that are said to have been the home to Vampires. Croglin Low Grange in Cumbria was mentioned in the memoirs of Augustus Hare as having a horrid vampire that each night would try to get in through the window. Whitby with famous for its links with Dracula also has a tall gentleman who stands in its hilltop graveyard. When you approach him, he simply disappears. The most notorious Vampire manifestation is at Highgate Cemetery in London, although every Halloween for the last forty years (since its last appearance) there has been huge security and a police presence.

From the Author

If you would like to submit an experience or was a witness to some of the stories in this book please email mj@mjwayland.com

Also for further ghost stories and research as well as my future releases please visit my website - www.mjwayland.com

Thank you

MJ Wayland

My other books include:

50 Real Ghost Stories
50 Real Ghost Stories 2
50 Real American Ghost Stories
Real Christmas Ghost Stories
The York Ghost Walk
The Derby Ghost Walk
Tales of the Polden Hills

All are available from Amazon and other good bookshops.

Printed in Great Britain
by Amazon